PERGAMON INTERNATIONAL LIBRARY
of Science, Technology, Engineering and Social Studies
*The 1000-volume original paperback library in aid of education,
industrial training and the enjoyment of leisure*
Publisher: Robert Maxwell, M.C.

MANAGEMENT CONTROL

SECOND EDITION

D1605626

THE PERGAMON TEXTBOOK
INSPECTION COPY SERVICE

An inspection copy of any book published in the Pergamon International Library
will gladly be sent to academic staff without obligation for their consideration for
course adoption or recommendation. Copies may be retained for a period of 60 days
from receipt and returned if not suitable. When a particular title is adopted or
recommended for adoption for class use and the recommendation results in a sale
of 12 or more copies, the inspection copy may be retained with our compliments.
If after examination the lecturer decides that the book is not suitable for adoption
but would like to retain it for his personal library, then a discount of 10% is
allowed on the invoiced price. The Publishers will be pleased to receive suggestions
for revised editions and new titles to be published in this important International
Library.

OMEGA Management Science Series

Editor:

PROFESSOR SAMUEL EILON

Other Titles in the Series

EILON, S.
Aspects of Management

EILON, S., GOLD, B. & SOESAN, J.
Applied Productivity Analysis for Industry

GOLD, B.
Technological Change: Economics, Management and Environment

KING, J. R.
Production Planning and Control: An Introduction to
Quantitative Methods

OMEGA

The International Journal of Management Science
Chief Editor: Professor Samuel Eilon
OMEGA keeps the practising manager informed of recent developments
in manpower planning, financial control, decision analysis, corporate
planning, organizational structure and design, management control,
technology and society, information systems and computers, and operational research.
Published bi-monthly
1979 subscription rate $115.00
Two years 1979/1980 $218.50

The terms of our inspection copy service apply to all the above books. Full details of
all books listed and specimen copies of journals listed will gladly be sent upon request.

MANAGEMENT CONTROL

by

SAMUEL EILON

Imperial College of Science and Technology, London

SECOND EDITION

PERGAMON PRESS

OXFORD · NEW YORK · TORONTO · SYDNEY · PARIS · FRANKFURT

U.K.	Pergamon Press Ltd., Headington Hill Hall, Oxford OX3 0BW, England
U.S.A.	Pergamon Press Inc., Maxwell House, Fairview Park, Elmsford, New York 10523, U.S.A.
CANADA	Pergamon of Canada Ltd., 75 The East Mall, Toronto, Ontario, Canada
AUSTRALIA	Pergamon Press (Aust.) Pty. Ltd., 19a Boundary Street, Rushcutters Bay, N.S.W. 2011, Australia
FRANCE	Pergamon Press SARL, 24 rue des Ecoles, 75240 Paris, Cedex 05, France
FEDERAL REPUBLIC OF GERMANY	Pergamon Press GmbH, 6242 Kronberg/Taunus, Pferdstrasse 1, Federal Republic of Germany

First edition 1971

Second edition 1979

British Library Cataloguing in Publication Data

Eilon, Samuel
Management control—2nd ed.—
(Omega management science series)—
(Omega management science)—
(Pergamon international library).
1. Management
I. Title   II. Omega management science series
658.4   HD31   78-40665
ISBN 0-08-022482-2 (Hard cover)
ISBN 0-08-022481-4 (Flexi cover)

Printed in Great Britain at the University Press, Aberdeen

To Hannah
who knows how to argue and
who is very often right

Preface

When the idea of writing a book on management control was suggested to me, my first reaction was that of reluctance. I confess that I have always found the vast literature on management theory and practice a serious obstacle in my studies in this field. The sheer amount of the material presented to us over the past two decades is bewildering enough, but it is not the amount alone that made me hesitate. On scanning through the literature it appears that almost every conceivable viewpoint has already been presented, almost every theoretical framework has been explored. The formidable array of knowledgeable and sophisticated authors that have made their mark on the literature should make anyone wonder whether there is anything significantly new to add to what has already been said.

And yet over the years I have become increasingly conscious of the fact that most treatises on management organisation and theory lack an adequate appreciation of the concept of *control* and the central role that it must play in the management task. This is not to say that control is completely ignored in the literature. Indeed, many writers devote lengthy passages to it. But with the exception of the few who have adopted a cybernetic approach, the term control is often superficially defined, sometimes even misused.

I have, therefore, decided to concentrate on particular aspects of management control. The book is not intended as a comprehensive textbook, nor is it an attempt to provide a critical review of the way in which the concept of control is treated in the literature. Where I quote other authors it is merely with the purpose of indicating agreement of approach or highlighting contrasting views and not with the intention of listing all the most relevant contributors to this subject.

Chapter 1 is devoted to identifying the management task as a control process, and several concepts relating to the management of systems and their organisation structure are introduced. The manager is seen as a controller of a system and his relationships with the system and with other controllers are therefore of fundamental importance to the design and maintenance of control procedures. These relationships are discussed in Chapters 2 and 3 and the special case of the two-state system is analysed in some detail in Chapter 4. Since the management process manifests itself in information flow through the system, Chapters 5 and 6 are devoted to information processing and to the discussion of various types of messages that are found in the system. Chapter 7 returns to the examination of the decision process and Chapter 8 discusses the extent to which decisions can become prescriptive and be affected by constraints. Chapter 9 continues to discuss the question of constraints and whether they should be distinguished from the proclaimed goals of the decision process and, finally, Chapter 10 includes some observations on theories of organisation structure.

Thus, the book has a limited objective, namely to discuss some of the important ingredients involved in the management process and to suggest fundamental concepts associated with the control function. My hope is that the discussion presented here will be of some value to students of management theory, irrespective of which discipline or school of thought they happen to represent.

The theme that runs through the book is that of the control function, but most of the chapters are self-contained and need not be read in the sequence presented. Some sections of the book (such as Chapter 2, pp. 77–85 and pp. 151–157) delve into technical details beyond the level of interest of the general reader, and these sections can be omitted without affecting his ability to understand the rest of the text. Also, various groups of students and practitioners may wish to concentrate only on certain parts of the book: students of organisation theory and behaviour will perhaps choose to omit Chapters 2–4, systems analysts should read Chapters 1 and 5–8, those with aptitude for the analysis of procedures will study Chapters 1–4 and 8, while senior managers may be interested in Chapters 1, 7 and 9–10.

This new edition is published in conjunction with the second edition of my book *Aspects of Management*, which is a collection of essays reflecting on current philosophies and practices in the management field. The two volumes may in some ways be regarded as complementary to each other, with *Management Control* concentrating on control procedures, information processing and decisions, while *Aspects of Management* is a more wide ranging discourse of organisational problems and methodologies. The themes of the last two chapters in this book, namely the implications of goals and constraints on the decision process and the degree of freedom or otherwise in the development of organisation structures, are pursued further in *Aspects of Management*. These are central themes of concern to students and practitioners alike, since they have a bearing on currently held organisation theories and on the validity of alternative approaches to organisational design.

In writing this book I have drawn heavily on several papers that I have written over the years and I am indebted to the editors of the following journals for permission to reproduce or quote extensively from those papers: *The International Journal of Production Research* (Chapter 1), *Nature* (Chapter 3), *Journal of Management Studies* (Chapters 2–5 and 8), *Administrative Science Quarterly* (Chapter 6) and *Management Science* (Chapter 7). I also owe a debt of gratitude to Professor Bela Gold for his friendship, encouragement and hospitality during my time as a Professorial Research Fellow in the Department of Economics and Case Western Reserve University in Cleveland, Ohio.

1979   S. E.

1*

Contents

1 Management, Systems and Control

DIVISION OF WORK

Management is as old as man. From time immemorial man has had to concern himself with the business of conducting his daily affairs, of employing his resources for given ends, of weighing alternative courses of action and making decisions. From time immemorial he has striven to build institutions for government, for administering law and order, for developing industry and commerce, for securing frontiers. And all these institutions are manifestations of man's aspiration to structure procedures with which he can manage his environment and control his destiny. Decision making and problems of management are not an invention of our present age; they have always been, and will always remain, part of human experience.

In Exodus 18 we find that when Jethro visited his son-in-law Moses he witnessed an occasion when Moses sat to judge the people 'and the people stood about Moses from morning unto the evening'. Jethro, who was probably one of the earliest management consultants on record, immediately perceived that Moses concentrated too much power in his own hands. 'Thou wilt surely wear away, both thou, and this people that is with thee: for the thing is too heavy for thee.' And Jethro proceeded to give his advice on how Moses could delegate authority[1]:

> thou shalt provide out of all the people able men, such as fear God, men of truth, hating unjust gain; and place such over them, to be rulers of thousands, rulers of hundreds, rulers of fifties, and rulers of tens. And let them judge the people at all seasons; and it shall be, that every great matter they shall bring unto thee, but every small matter they shall judge themselves; so shall they make it easier for thee and bear the burden with thee.

Delegation is, indeed, one of the central themes in the practice of management. As man's span of activities widens, as his horizon and aspirations expand; as the task of controlling the activities of groups becomes

1

intricate, man finds it more and more difficult to be omnipotent on his own and increasingly he has to rely on others to help in the task of management.

The principle of the division of labour was postulated by Adam Smith, who started the first chapter of his book by saying[2]:

> The greatest improvement in the productive powers of labour, and the greater skill, dexterity, and judgement with which it is anywhere directed or applied, seems to have been the effects of the division of labour.

Adam Smith devoted his discussion mainly to production activities in manufacturing industries (his Book I was entitled: 'Of the causes of improvement in the productive powers of labour, and of the order according to which its produce is naturally distributed among the different ranks of the people') and this is probably why the principle of the division of labour has always been associated in people's minds with production work on the shop floor.

Division of work may perhaps be identified in three categories:

1. *By skill or trade*—certain tasks or operations are assigned to one worker while others are assigned to another; in this way the worker who specialises in a particular craft is able to perform the task more efficiently than a man of all trades.

2. *By sequence of operations*—the operations may not entail skills which the worker needs a long time to acquire, but the flow of work and materials makes it desirable to break down the operations according to their sequence, each worker receiving materials required only for his own task; assembly lines in mass or large batch production are examples of this type of division of work.

3. *By physical locations*—a group of workers or a department is assigned to its own range of tasks or products, the idea being that if several groups in different locations are assigned identical tasks the outcome may help to reduce distribution costs; admittedly, such a scheme has the possible disadvantage of dissipating opportunities for developing specialised skills, of inefficient use of plant and of missing possible opportunities of economies of scale.

The concept of division of work also pervades the realm of management and the three types of division that were suggested for production work can be discerned here as well. There is division according to skill; staff functions; professional expertise. There is division in time: separate procurement, production and marketing functions; separate companies, each engaged in a distinct part of the conversion process from raw materials to finished goods, all these companies being joined in what is called 'vertical integration'. And there is geographical division: subsidiary companies for regional coverage; product divisions.

But division of work is not synonymous with delegation. The first implies some degree of equality of responsibility for the work done by the constituent contributors. If work is divided between A and B, then we expect each to be responsible for the work assigned to him. This does not mean, of course, that A and B are equal in status or that their respective tasks are equally important or equally difficult. It merely means that in assigning work the principle of divisibility is recognised, that if C decides to divide work between A and B then A is accountable for the task apportioned to him and not for the task given to B, and similarly B cannot be held responsible for the task assigned to A. It is in this sense that A and B are equal, namely that the division of work does not necessarily involve hierarchical relationships between them.

Delegation, however, does imply a hierarchical relationship. Delegation is the entrusting of authority and responsibility, so that if A delegates work to B, the latter acts *on behalf* of the former and is accountable to the former for his actions. In delegating work, A does not relinquish his responsibility; thus, while B is held responsible for the work with which he is entrusted but cannot be made accountable for A's actions, A can be made accountable for B's actions. In division of work there is no region of overlapping responsibilities between the respective performers of the divided tasks; delegation, however, implies transference of responsibility, and furthermore this transference is unidirectional, from the delegator to the delegatee, and not in the opposite direction.

When A delegates work to B his purpose is to secure help in completing the task assigned to him. He may decide to delegate either because he lacks certain technical skills which B possesses, or because he has many duties to attend to and is unable to complete them in time on his own. Whatever the reason, as soon as A delegates a task to B he expects B to complete the task for him and he divests himself of the need to do the task himself. But he does not divest himself of responsibility for the task. To comprehend the full import of these statements perhaps we need to examine the concepts of authority and responsibility more closely.

POWER, AUTHORITY, RESPONSIBILITY, ACCOUNTABILITY

The literature on management theory and practice abounds with discussions and arguments on *power, authority, responsibility* and *accountability*. Much of the polemics is evidently rooted in the problem of suggesting concise and unambiguous definitions for these terms, and it is sometimes difficult to ascertain to what extent the seemingly wide divergence of views expressed by various authors is due merely to semantics rather than ingrained social attitudes.

I believe that the following definitions represent the consensus of opinion of many writers, but I am conscious of the fact that others may disapprove (some on a question of detail, others more fundamentally) of the implications of these definitions:

> *Power*—the ability to take action to effect a change in one's environ-ment or in someone else's environment
> *authority*—the acknowledged right to command, to make decisions or take action
> *responsibility*—the obligation to act in given circumstances in a given way
> *accountability*—the obligation to explain and justify one's actions.

An interesting discussion of the concept of *power* can be found in Gross.[3] He develops the proposition that power can be identified as a cause–effect relationship. Power is the ability to influence the course of events and in order to ascertain that such an influence exists there is a need to examine the instances in which the exercise of power is manifest in results that can be attributed to it. Gross also points out that

> the concept (of power) may be used in the sense of either the *actual* or the *potential*. Actual (or kinetic) power is the production of certain re-sults. Potential power is the capacity to bring about certain results.[4]

Authority is generally defined as the legal or acknowledged right to command or to take action and, as Barnard[5] asserts, for authority to exist there is a need for acceptance by others that an individual may exercise the right to command. Without such an acceptance, authority cannot exist. In his discussion of the role of authority Simon lists three functions of authority that deserve a special mention:

1. It (authority) enforces responsibility of the individual to those who wield the authority;
2. It secures expertise in the making of decisions;
3. It permits coordination of activity.[6]

Paterson[7] distinguishes between *structural authority*, which is 'the en-titlement to command . . . and to expect obedience in the ordering and coordinating', and *sapiential authority*, which is vested in the person and implies 'requisite knowledge of the function'. The former is impersonal and is determined by what is thought the powers of a given position in the structure should have, while the latter is associated with a particular person, when his authority is attributed to his technical knowledge rather than his position.

Paterson also discusses responsibility and accountability at great length and tries to draw sharp distinctions between them. He defines responsibility as 'a relation between moral agents, one acting, and the other exercising structural authority, judging action and imposing retribution for failure', whereas accountability to him is 'the relation between two persons, both of whom are responsible to a third, and in which one is expected, as of right, but is not obliged to obey the orders of the other'. Paterson draws on many examples from military organisations and concludes that 'responsibility entails accountability but accountability does not entail responsibility'.

I am inclined to follow Gross[4] in his distinction between *responsibility for* and *responsibility to*. The first is an obligation to perform a task, the second is a description of a hierarchical relationship. If A is responsible *for* a given task *to* B then he is expected to carry out his duties and to act whenever circumstances require actions on his part, and he is also obliged to keep B informed and to explain his actions to B. *Responsibility for* is in relation to certain tasks; *responsibility to* is in relation to someone who has the authority to inquire into one's actions and who expects to receive appropriate explanations.

Thus, when I am told that a person is held responsible I expect him to ensure that an array of activities which have been assigned to him are accomplished in accordance with given rules and specifications. To this end he is accountable for his actions.

Accountability involves the need to provide a reasoned justification for one's action. This often takes the form of a diagnosis of the circumstances and an elucidation of the action taken and the outcome of this action. I therefore regard responsibility as inextricably bound with accountability. To give a person responsibility and not make him accountable is to create a situation in which it is impossible to evaluate his actions. He may make good decisions or bad ones, he may even exceed his authority, but unless he is accountable, no judgement regarding his behaviour can be made. On the other hand, accountability without responsibility implies the need to keep under review the activities of individuals and therefore in this sense every individual in an organisation is accountable. This does not mean, of course, that everyone is required to record in great detail everything that he does and send a periodic report to his superior, but it does mean that everyone *may* be called upon to explain and justify his actions. I, therefore, accept Paterson's statement that 'responsibility entails accountability but accountability does not entail responsibility', even though our definitions of these terms do not coincide.

One aspect of the differences in definitions stems, in my view, from the need to distinguish between *command authority* and *judicial authority*. Command authority is the right to take action, or give instructions and to expect that instructions are carried out satisfactorily (and in the main this is what is meant by the term 'authority' in this book). Judicial authority is to do with meting out rewards and punishments. In many organisational relationships the two types of authority are combined in the same person, but they need not be, and very often one finds that while the person who holds command authority may initiate and continue to be an important component in judicial proceedings, he is not authorised to make decisions on his own about rewards and punishments. This is perhaps the essence of Paterson's 'triadic system', in which (in his terms) '*A* may be accountable to *B* but responsible to *C*', if *C* and not *B* can 'enforce' (through punishment) the obedience of *A*, and Paterson quotes the relationships of the private–sergeant–officer in the military organisation to illustrate his point. However, if the question of judicial authority is defined and described in an organisation structure quite separately from command authority, any ambivalence in a responsibility relationship versus accountability relationship immediately disappears. As I have already suggested, some of these differences in definitions may be regarded as purely semantic.

Another consequence of these differences relates to the question of freedom of action. Paterson[7] argues at some length that 'to be held responsible, a man is given, and contracts to assume, the freedom to make a choice'. But following the definitions of responsibility and accountability suggested here (and the distinction between command authority and judicial authority), the question of freedom of action is quite irrelevant to responsibility. Even if a person is given no alternative courses of action at all and is told precisely how to act in every circumstance, he can still be held responsible for following instructions. He may decide, of course, to opt out altogether, if he strongly objects to having been put in this strait-jacket, or if there is a serious conflict between the prescribed action and his conscience. It is only in this sense that this person can be said to have a choice. But if he does not opt out, he has no alternative but to act as prescribed. If a failure occurs, he may be asked to account for his actions, and the fact that he has merely followed instructions and has no authority to do otherwise may well exonerate him and result in the person who has issued the instructions having to provide an explanation. One could argue that it may be inadvisable to give someone responsibility without some freedom of choice, but this is, of course, quite different from the proposition that freedom of choice must be a requisite to assigning responsibility.

DELEGATION OF AUTHORITY AND RESPONSIBILITY

Paul Getty, the oilman, is reported to have said: 'I believe in delegating work, but I'm president of the company and as president you have certain responsibility you can't delegate. You can delegate work, but you can't delegate responsibility'.[8] This idea that responsibility cannot be delegated pervades the literature on management theory and practice, as illustrated by a similar remark by Paterson[7] that a manager can delegate authority but he cannot delegate responsibility 'because it cannot be cut up and bits and pieces passed on to somebody else'. There is this idea that delegation of responsibility must imply that responsibility is a divisible entity, that once the whole is divided into several parts, there is a need to assign a label of ownership to each part. Work is generally treated in this way. When work study engineers analyse an operation they divide it into separate elements and subsequently they combine elements, perhaps in different sequences, thereby implicitly following the conservation of work principle: the sum of the constituent parts equals the whole and is not a function of the way in which the whole is divided. Thus, when A delegates work, he no longer needs to carry out the tasks which he has delegated. It is to avoid the idea that he is also no longer responsible for delegated work that the maxim that responsibility cannot be delegated has been suggested.

However, if responsibility cannot be delegated, how can anyone in an organisation have it? Does a person assume responsibility on his own, without any hierarchical sanction, and if so under what circumstances does he and can he assume such responsibility? I also find it difficult to conceive of someone being asked to carry out a task and yet not be made responsible for it. Does it mean that he is not accountable for the way in which the task is carried out? If he is not accountable, then how can one ensure that the task is performed properly? It is only by making him accountable that higher authority can judge his performance and indeed decide whether to make changes in future allocation of duties; and it is only by making him responsible for the task that action can be taken by the appropriate judicial authority, when such action is considered to be desirable. How can this argument be reconciled with the suggestion that responsibility cannot be delegated, because of the need for higher authority to be held responsible for actions taken in the lower echelons of the organisation structure?

The solution to this dilemma is, of course, to abandon the notion of conservation of responsibility. If a manager delegates .work, and with it responsibility, to another person, his own work load is thereby diminished, but his responsibility is not. The interpretation that should, therefore, be attributed to the maxim about delegation of responsibility is that *a manager cannot divest himself of responsibility by delegation.*

As indicated earlier, delegation implies a hierarchical relationship, which is the essence of organisation structures. A manager may be able to delegate any given task to another, but not *vice versa*. Delegation is unidirectional; so is accountability, except that it operates in the opposite direction to delegation.

The arguments put forward by various writers for the proposition that responsibility cannot be delegated perhaps stem from, or at least are influenced by, the writings of Follett, although her concern was not so much the delegation of responsibility as the question of delegation of power or authority. 'I do not think that power can be delegated' she wrote and added:[9] 'You cannot confer power, because power is the blossoming of experience'. She suggested that her concept of authority and responsibility 'should do away with the idea almost universally held that the president *delegates* authority and responsibility'. Again, there seems to be this concern that delegation implies diminution of the authority of the delegator, and because she sees authority as emanating from the function or the position of the manager in the organisation structure, she cannot conceive of delegation of authority except when the manager is ill or takes a vacation (and even then 'you have not exactly delegated authority. Someone is doing your work and he has the authority that goes with that particular piece of work'[9]).

It would have been a simple matter to brush aside this argument by suggesting that the term 'delegation of authority' should be interpreted in the same light as 'delegation of responsibility', namely that no diminution of the authority of the delegator is implied. I believe, however, that such a diminution can and does occur, and that in some circumstances it is even inevitable. If we regard authority as the acknowledged right to take action, then in relation to a given task one's freedom and ability to take action may be curtailed if authority pertaining to the same task is delegated to someone else. The whole purpose of delegation of authority is to allow the delegator to recede from the scene of action, so that he need no longer react each time an action is called for—someone else is reacting for him. When A delegates authority to B, A may wish to retain the ability to intervene at any time and supersede decisions or actions taken by B, but in reality he may not always be able to do so. For one thing, there is the time and place factor: the nature of delegation may be such that by the time A receives information it is too late for him to act and only B may be able to act in time. It may be physically impossible for A to scan and vet all B's decisions with the view of intervening when required, because if this vetting is to be carried out before B's decisions are executed, too much time may be lost in the process, and if the vetting is to be undertaken after the decisions are executed then it may be too late for A to reverse a decision. In the latter case he can only *evaluate decisions after the event*, but he has lost the ability to take action at the time when such action is needed, and in this sense he has lost power and authority in relation to the particular task for which authority has been delegated to B.

The nature of delegation may be such that even when there is ample time, A simply does not get to know about some of B's decisions at the time when intervention is possible. In Chapter 3 some problems of linkages between controllers of a system are discussed at some length and the discussion suggests that certain linkages express hierarchical relationships involving delegation of authority whereby B acts on behalf of A in such a way that only some of B's decisions are referred to A for ratification. Under such circumstances it is inevitable that A must concede that some of his authority with respect to a given task is surrendered to B. It is, of course, quite possible that as a result of such delegation A is able to have responsibility for more tasks, to have more people accountable to him and generally to have his status and overall power and authority greatly enhanced. But in relation to a given task or an array of tasks, looked at in isolation, A may lose some of his authority when he delegates authority to B.

It seems to me, therefore, that the term *delegation* should not be regarded as having a single meaning. Delegation of work, delegation of authority, delegation of responsibility, all have different connotations:

Delegation of work. The principle of conservation of work generally applies, so that delegation involves transfer of work and the delegator expects a reduction of his own workload by the amount transferred.

Delegation of authority. There is no conservation of the amount of authority in the system and when authority is delegated the delegator retains the right, though not always the ability, to intervene. A diminution of the authority of the delegator may well occur with respect to the range of duties for which authority is delegated.

Delegation of responsibility. When work or authority are delegated a corresponding delegation of responsibility must be implied. Unlike the other two, however, delegation of responsibility results in no diminution of the responsibility of the delegator.

MANAGEMENT AND ORGANISATION STRUCTURE

'The art of management has been defined', wrote Taylor,[10] 'as knowing exactly what you want men to do, and then seeing that they do it in the best and cheapest way. No concise definition can fully describe an art, but the relations between employers and men form without question the most important part of this art'. A more elaborate definition is given by Brech:[11]

> Management is a social process entailing responsibility for the effective (or efficient) planning or regulation of the operations of the enterprise in fulfilment of a given purpose or task, such responsibility involving (a) the installation and maintenance of proper procedures to ensure adherence to plans, and (b) the guidance, integration and supervision of the personnel comprising the enterprise and carrying out is operations.

One could argue that this definition is probably too vague in certain respects, or one could disagree with points of emphasis (it could be suggested, for example, that more prominence should be given to the decision-making function of the manager), but the definition of Brech does convey the essential elements of the management task: *the need to establish control procedures* and *the need to define, and indeed to understand, relationships between people in the enterprise.*

The latter element manifests itself in the organisation structure, which identifies the major tasks of groups in the enterprise, their hierarchical relationships and their responsibilities; the former—the control function—provides solutions to problems that these groups or individuals are likely to encounter in the course of performing their tasks. An organisation structure is the body of the enterprise, control is its soul. The one cannot exist without the other.

This is why so much criticism has been levelled at the organisation chart in recent years. The chart is an attempt to provide a description—albeit a limited one—of the structure. Even if the chart succeeds in this task, it tells only part of the story. For one thing, the chart is just a static graphic network of hierarchical echelons and channels of communications. It does not depict how particular tasks that management is required to perform should be handled; it does not indicate how an individual manager (or a department) is supposed to solve problems; it does not give an observer a clue as to the various steps and sequential activities that are involved in the decision-making process. To gain an insight into these issues we must turn to the control function.

This is not to say that organisation structure and control are independent of each other. Sometimes it is necessary to use control procedures that hardly provide a structural choice. The time allowed for action may be so tightly specified, or the kind of analysis of data required prior to a decision may be so rigidly defined, that perhaps only one particular structure will fit the bill. Similarly, a line of demarcation between functions as defined by a given structure, or the position of a given individual within the structure, may lead to the institution of certain procedures and rule out the adoption of others. It is wrong, however, to conclude that by studying the structure one is likely to obtain a clear picture of how control is exercised, although the converse is probably more likely, namely that by studying the control function one may make many inferences about the structure.

BEHAVIOUR

The existence of an organisation is a manifestation of the fact that an individual or a group of people wish to attain a certain objective, such as the manufacture of certain products or the provision of given services. The individual or the group are faced with the problem: how is this task that we wish to perform to be carried out? And the answer is: by setting up an organisation, in which the total task is subdivided into several identifiable entities and these are assigned to various parts of the organisation and to the people involved. The organisation requires a structure, in which relationships between individuals and groups are defined or evolve and this leads to behavioural characteristics that can be observed. The simple model which describes this development is shown in Figure 1.1

ACTIVITY ⟶ ORGANISATION ⟶ BEHAVIOUR

Figure 1.1   Too simple a model for the cause of behaviour

This notion of a unidirectional cause and effect relationship is an over-simplification. It is probably more realistic to consider the original global task as a part of the general environment and to recognise that in the triad which consists of the environment, the organisation and behaviour there are influences and responses which operate in both directions (as in Figure 1.2). The environment, which encompasses the social and economic system within which companies have a function, creates a set of potential requirements for goods and services and this set provides the enterprise a framework within which to define its goals and tasks.

The environment, external and internal, affects the organisation, its structure and the control procedures which it will employ, and the organisation has an effect on behaviour, whether it is the global behaviour of the organisation as a whole, or groups or even individuals within it. The three categories of behaviour have an effect on each other and in turn on the structure and the control procedures of the enterprise. And the environment, although generally slower to react and to change than firms and individuals do, is eventually affected by what happens in individual firms.

The concept of the triad in Figure 1.2 is that of constant adaptation. Each part of the triad needs to adapt to changes that occur in the other parts, and as the various parts are subject to different rates of change and have very different inertia and response-time characteristics, conflicts are bound constantly to emerge.

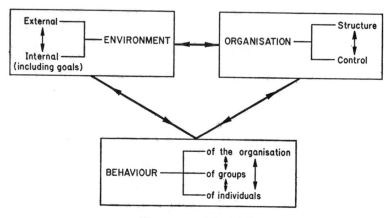

Figure 1.2   The triad

The triad in Figure 1.2 also represents the multitude of possible approaches to the problem of studying organisations. First there are economists and political scientists, who mainly concern themselves with studies of the environment, the way it imposes constraints on individual firms, the way in which it allows certain industries to develop and others to contract. Economists are also interested in the scale of operations, in growth patterns, in cost ratios between labour and plant and in their implications on competition and the scope of operations. Then there are economists and accountants, who look at a variety of financial ratios and proceed to make comparisons between firms. Then there are technologists, who are particularly interested in methods and machinery, in design, in research and development, in materials and quality. Sociologists are interested in the behaviour of groups and psychologists in the behaviour of individuals.

Understandably, these various approaches rarely transcend the primary disciplines that students of management come from, and this is clearly expressed in the many different viewpoints found in the literature. For the behavioural scientists, for example, the study of organisations is the study of behaviour, graphically expressed in such terms as 'organisational behaviour'. But the term 'organisational behaviour' is somewhat vague. It may either mean the behaviour of the organisation, or it may mean behaviour (of groups or of individuals) characterised by the effects of the organisation. Most books on this subject appear to adopt the latter interpretation and rarely consider the organisation as a whole. Indeed, the first interpretation raises many difficulties if the term 'behaviour' is to be regarded strictly from the behavioural scientist's viewpoint. What does it precisely mean? There are, of course, various ways of describing group behaviour, but the assumption is that the group provides a bond between the members of the group sufficiently strong to allow the behaviour of the group to be characterised in some form. Can this assumption be extended to the organisation as a whole? If an organisation consists of several groups, which are heterogeneous in their character, can one discern a common denominator of behaviour of the various groups that may be identified as the behaviour of the organisation? It seems that in the context of human behaviour the first interpretation of organisational behaviour remains unsatisfactory, and in many ways even misleading.

If, however, the term behaviour is viewed with connotations of performance and response, then the behaviour of the organisation may be regarded in the same way as the behaviour of a system. Engineers, for example, often refer to the behaviour of mechanisms and systems, and what they have in mind is not human behaviour but the way in which systems respond and operate under given conditions. The behaviour of the enterprise may be expressed in terms which economists and engineers are familiar with, using various measures of performance and input–output analyses.

Thus, in the area of behaviour there are different levels at which studies can be conducted, and this is perhaps analogous to different levels of analysis encountered in the physical sciences. In the study of materials, for example, the scientist can address himself to what may be termed 'macro' phenomena by examining the physical properties of materials and the nature of their response to external forces; or he may study the molecular or atomic structure of materials from the 'micro' angle. Similarly, in the study of organisations it is possible to single out the organisation as a whole, or to observe parts of it (the study of the behaviour of groups is an approach generally advocated by sociologists), or to concentrate on the behaviour of individuals within the organisation (which is what social psychologists tend to do).

The result is a plethora of books and articles on the subject of management theory and it becomes a gigantic task for anyone who attempts to provide a comparative account of all that has been written on the subject. The mammoth work of Gross,[3] which consists of almost 1000 pages and many hundreds of references, is an example of the enormity of the task involved, and it requires a collection of numerous individual contributions, such as the compilation of March[12] in the *Handbook of Organisations* to provide anything like a representative review of the various schools of thought in this field.

MANAGEMENT CONTROL

This book is not an attempt to review the literature, nor does it even pretend to render a critical assessment of the 'state of the art'. It puts forward the proposition that among the many different but valid approaches to management theory there is a need to present the concept of control as a ubiquitous element in the management process. Indeed, it must be evident that control, with its primary characteristics of feedback and corrective action, is a fundamental and an indispensible part of the management task. Without control there can be no management. This book is, therefore, concerned with management control, with relationships between controllers which are expressed in procedural terms, and with the decision making process.

The term *control* is somewhat loosely employed in the management literature. Control is often associated with financial matters (the role of comptrollers in organisations is familiar enough), with production and inventory (the terms 'production control' and 'inventory control' are in common use), but more rarely with other managerial functions. This is somewhat surprising, since most dictionaries provide fairly good and not too ambiguous definitions. The Oxford English Dictionary, for example, states (among other definitions) that control is 'power or authority to direct and govern; a standard for comparing and testing'. Also the field of control engineering, which is particularly concerned with the behaviour of control mechanisms and the way they affect the systems that they control, may be helpful in defining concepts relating to managerial control situations.

Servo-mechanism theory tells us that control is associated with an adjustment, namely with a corrective action designed to guide the system to function to a predetermined standard. A governor of a steam engine, a navigator of a ship, a driver of a car—all are controllers of their respective systems: the governor regulates the speed of the engine, the navigator steers the ship to a given course, and the driver follows a certain route and keeps to some specified distance from the kerb.

No corrective action is possible without feedback. The purpose of feedback is to provide information about the way the system is operating, so that the discrepancy between actual performance and the desirable level of performance can be assessed. When this discrepancy has been determined, the controller decides whether to take action or not. The discrepancy may be too small for him to bother about, in which case it could be completely ignored by the controller and the system would be none the wiser. If the discrepancy is too large to tolerate, the controller reacts, and the system responds to his command in a suitable way. The controller may therefore be defined as that component in the system that has the ability deliberately to adjust or change the system's performance.

There is no reason why such concepts may not be used in the study of administrative systems. The manager is a controller of a system. He monitors and analyses the performance of the system under his charge in the same way that a governor of a steam engine keeps watch on engine speed and the way a driver controls his car. The car driver is in fact a manager of a system, the car. He has an objective, to get to a given destination, and he monitors various performance characteristics associated with the car (such as the speed, the distance from the kerb and from other cars) and decides when to adjust the performance by the use of various control levers. The manager of a system who sits in an office essentially operates in the same way.

The concept of feedback is fundamental, of course. If a driver of a car drives in pitch dark without lights and without any means of identifying the position of the road, how can he steer the car? Similarly, if a manager has no information about the way his team or department is performing, how can he manage?

Some people may find it disturbing, perhaps even distasteful, that the notion of resemblances between inanimate control mechanisms and humans should be entertained. Sir Geoffrey Vickers once wrote:[13] 'In the days when our minds were dominated by mechanical analogies, industry was inclined to think of men as cogs in a machine. It is probably no less misleading to think of them as relays.' Sir Geoffrey was not denigrating the use of the control concept (in fact on the same page he suggested that the effect of movements in stock prices on buying or selling is 'as surely as a Watts governor opens or closes a valve'), but his statement is reminiscent of the strong criticisms so often levelled at the Taylor school of thought (dating back to the beginning of the century) for its mechanistic outlook of the management task. Of course men are not relays. But there must be certain fundamental elements of the control function that are both essential and valid, irrespective of whether the controller is a human being or a mechanical device.

SYSTEMS

Lee[14] suggests four classes of man-made systems (man-made systems are 'purposively designed' by man, as opposed to natural systems, which are part of nature): procedural, physical, social and conceptual. A procedural system is a collection of relative rules and procedures set up to help in decision making or problem solving; a physical system is a collection of physical elements connected or assembled for a given purpose; a social system is a group of people working together or banding together for a common purpose; a conceptual system is a theory, or a model.

A system is a set of elements between which there exist relationships that can be described by formal statements. The group of planets revolving round the sun is a system; the Milky Way is a system; an internal combustion engine is a system; and so is a production department, a machine shop, a design office, or indeed a whole enterprise In each case the elements that comprise the system can be enumerated, and certain relationships between the elements can be expressed.

Every system can be subdivided into subsystems and can also be combined with other systems to form a larger system. An enterprise can be subdivided into departments, each department into working groups, each group to individual man–machine systems. Also, an enterprise is part of an industry, and the industry is part of a national economic system, and so on. The two extremes of the spectrum are elementary particles on the one hand and the universe on the other.

In thermodynamics a distinction is made between open systems and closed systems. An open system is one for which there is a flow of materials or energy across the boundaries of the system, whereas in a closed system such a flow does not occur. This distinction allows general statements to be made about the properties of closed systems, for example on conservation of matter and energy, or on entropy having to increase with time. Such generalisations are naturally useful in the study of open systems, where account can be taken of material and energy flow across the boundaries. Many systems that man has an interest in are open systems, and this category includes living organisms and industrial enterprises.

One of the problems that faces an investigator of an industrial system is drawing boundaries around it. As in physical systems, there are no hard and fast rules. Boundaries are a matter of convenience, certainly in the case of open systems, and express the interests of the investigator. There is no *a priori* reason to suggest that particular definitions are the only valid ones, and provided the definitions are compatible with the objective of the investigation, there are often several choices open to the investigator. This, incidentally, often results in studies undertaken by various investigators not being entirely comparable, not just because of the different research and observation methods employed, but because the systems under study are very different in their definitions.

THE CONTROL PROCESS

A simple closed-loop control process is described in Figure 1.3. A system is assigned a particular task to perform, say to manufacture a given product. The target requirement is specified and the appropriate signal θ_i is transmitted to the system. In a production system this signal may indicate the rate of production that the system is expected to work at. In reality the system may yield an output θ_0 and a recording device (such as a human observer, a mechanical counter, a production report) makes a note of this fact and informs the controller that a discrepancy, or an error, amounting to $\varepsilon = \theta_i - \theta_0$ exists between the target and the output level.

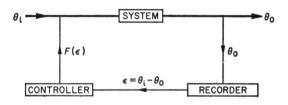

Figure 1.3   A simple control process

The controller digests this feedback signal and decides on an appropriate course of action which takes the form of a fresh instruction to the system through a signal $F(\varepsilon)$. This new signal is a function of the error ε. In some circumstances the controller may choose to ignore the error signal altogether, for example when he believes that the discrepancy between the required output and the actual output is merely due to chance variations. In other cases, particularly when there is a time lag between the moment that information on output is available and the moment that the controller is made aware of the performance of the system, he may be inclined to 'overcompensate' (in other words, to instruct the system to change its level of performance by more than ε) in order to account for the cumulative discrepancies during the time lag.

The illustration described in Figure 1.3 highlights the following essential ingredients of any closed loop control process:

- a goal, or standard
- a measurement task
- a feedback signal
- a control procedure
- a corrective action

First, there must be a goal, or a standard of performance. In Figure 1.3

the standard is denoted by θ_i—this is the level at which the system is required to operate. Then there is a measurement activity that strives to determine the actual level of performance of the system. This measurement, coupled with a comparison with the standard, enables the recorder to send a signal to the controller, and this feedback signal provides vital information to the controller before he decides what to do. The controller is armed with a set of instructions which tell him how to react in various circumstances, or he may be required to evaluate the information on his own and use his own discretion as to the appropriate action that should be adopted. And finally, the controller issues an instruction which describes the corrective action that the system should take.

Notice that each of these ingredients is a vital link in the chain of control. If one fails, the whole control process fails. If there is no standard, or if there is no measurement activity, there is no way in which reliable information can be fed to the control mechanism about the degree to which the system conforms to the original schedule or mode of operations. Similarly, the failure of a feedback signal to reach the controller means that the preceding measurement effort has been completely wasted, and incidentally this is what happens only too often in administrative systems where elaborate records are compiled only to be carefully filed away in meticulously organised archives, while managers are deprived of essential and available information with which to control activities under their charge. The control procedures are designed to guide the controller in his task. They provide him with solutions to a variety of problems that he is likely to face in the course of his work, so that he need not seek fresh solutions in recurring situations. Thus, the control procedures attempt to ensure that consistency of reaction is maintained and that circumstances covered by the procedures are not likely to be handled differently when the controller is replaced.

The term 'controller' is often used to describe the decision maker, namely the element that transmits a signal for corrective action. In some ways this is unfortunate. To many it may have the implication that the control function is confined to the task of the decision maker, whereas it is important to realise that the decision box is just an element—albeit an essential one—in the control process, which encompasses all the stages described in Figure 1.3. Admittedly, the use of the word 'controller' in this book is somewhat ambivalent, sometimes it refers to the person in charge of the whole control process, sometimes (in accordance with more common usage) it has the narrower connotation depicted by the decision box in Figure 1.3, but I hope that this will not result in any ambiguity in interpreting the role of the controller in each case.

Two important facets of the control process that are not apparent from

Figure 1.3 are *system reaction* and *time lag*. System reaction, as the term implies, depicts the way in which a system reacts to the input. This reaction may depend on one or several of the following characteristics:

- the signal
- exogenous parameters
- endogenous parameters

First, the signal. The reaction of the system may depend on the type of signal and indeed on its content. If the signal generated by the decision maker calls for a drastic change in the level of performance of the system, the discrepancy between the actual and the desired levels of performance may be greater than when the change that is called for is comparatively moderate. Secondly, there is the possible effect of exogenous variables, for example the properties of the physical input to the system (such as the quality characteristics of raw materials or semi-finished goods). Thirdly, the reaction of the system may well depend on its internal structure and composition, the properties of the physical facilities that are put at its disposal, and the attributes of the manpower that constitutes part of the system.

Superimposed on these, the system reaction may have deterministic or stochastic characteristics. A deterministic reaction implies that the system always reacts in the same way to a given set of circumstances, so that when the circumstances are known in advance it is possible to forecast accurately how the system will behave. There are many systems, however, which do not react in a deterministic fashion and where it is necessary to employ probability values to describe the possible response of the system to any given set of input parameters.

The other important facet of the control process is time lag. Time lag may occur at every single stage of the process: there may be a delay in measurement and recording, or in transmitting a feedback signal to the decision maker, or in the decision maker making up his mind about his next move. There may be delays in the transmission channels of communication because of their design and the volume of information that they have to cope with. And, of course, there may be a delay in the system's response to instructions and to external stimuli. Some of these time lags may have deterministic characteristics, others may be variable, but to ensure that control is effective it is necessary to take account of these time lags in designing the appropriate procedures.

The behaviour of the system and the set of characteristics by which this behaviour can be identified define the state of the system. As circumstances change and as the system reacts to the environment and to the controller's instructions, it moves from one state to another. If the time dimension is divided into discrete intervals, the state of system at interval $n + 1$ may be described as

$$S_{n+1} = f(S_n, D_n, E_n, F_n) \qquad (1)$$

where S_{n+1} is the state of the system in interval $n + 1$

   S_n is the state of the system in interval n

   D_n is the decision of the controller in interval n; it represents the set of updated instructions to the system (instructions issued prior to interval n, as well as modifications and new instructions added in interval n)

   E_n is the set of endogenous variables that define the interval environment, including changes in the operating structure of the system

   F_n is the set of characteristics that describe the external environment.

Thus, in addition to the effect of the controller and that of the internal and external environment, the state of the system is also a function of its previous state, and this represents the notion of inertia and resistance to change. In this formulation the time lag for response is assumed to be uniform for all the variables and to correspond to one time interval, but the functional relationship can be suitably modified if several time lags are involved.

GOAL SEEKING

In his efforts to develop a general system theory, Mesarovic suggests various concepts for multi-level multi-goal systems.[15,16] Starting with a single-level single-goal system, Mesarovic makes a distinction between a system and a goal-seeking unit, as shown in Figure 1.4. The system, which he calls the 'causal part' has a certain input (say, of raw materials) which is converted by the system to an output. A goal-seeking unit receives information about the way the system performs and about its output, and as it is motivated to attain a given goal ('which is either externally or internally generated'), the goal-seeking unit takes action and issues instructions to modify the working of the system. Thus, there are two classes of behaviour phenomena: the behaviour of the system (the way it reacts to the input and to instructions) and the behaviour of the goal-seeking unit (the way it reacts to information about the way the system behaves).

These concepts are very similar to the scheme shown in Figure 1.3. The goal-seeking unit is none other than the decision maker (or controller) in Figure 1.3. The measurement activity described in Figure 1.3 can be incorporated in the system or in the decision maker, and in either case the result is shown in Figure 1.4.

If a system is defined in such a way that it consists of the 'causal part' and of the goal-seeking unit, as shown by the broken line in Figure 1.4, then we have a *teleological* (= goal seeking) *system*. A system which changes its internal structure in response to changes in the input is called a *self-organising system* and a *teleological self-organising system* is one that changes its structure in pursuit of its goal and in response to changes in

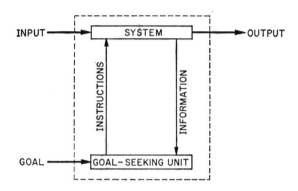

Figure 1.4 A single-level single-goal system

input. In all these cases learning may be involved. In the simple example of Figure 1.4 an opportunity for learning and adapting is available to the goal-seeking unit; in a teleological self-organising system, the system as a whole seeks to optimise its internal structure as a means of attaining optimal performance.

Figures 1.3 and 1.4 describe a simple case, in which a single controller has a single goal that he wishes to attain. Such a situation rarely occurs in practice. It is far more common, particularly in administrative systems, to encounter various interactions between several controllers, some with very different goals in mind.

Mesarovic discusses the concept of a multi-level system, in which several subsystems are grouped in a given hierarchy. Two goal-seeking units A and B are considered to be on a different level if, say, A can directly affect B, but not *vice versa*. A is then called *supremal* to B while B is *infimal* to A. The infimal may, of course, have an ultimate effect on the supremal, but only indirectly, namely the infimal affects the behaviour of the system and in turn this affects the supremal. The effect of a

2+

supremal on an infimal is called direct intervention, which may be in
three forms:

1. *Goal intervention*—the supremal effects a direct change in the goal of
   the infimal.
2. *Information intervention*—the supremal provides the infimal with
   information designed to improve the infimal's behaviour from the
   supremal's standpoint.
3. *Constraints intervention*—the supremal restricts the freedom of action
   of the infimal.

In a multi-level system there are three types of units: the highest level
unit (to which there is no supremal), the intermediate unit (which has
both a supremal and an infimal) and the first-level unit (to which there is
no infimal).

The multi-goal system represents the situation where several goals are
sought and some may even be in conflict. The theory of games is cited by
Mesarovic as an example of an analysis of a competitive situation, in
which several decision makers are in competition in what may be described as a single-level multi-goal system. Mesarovic *et al.*[16] argue that an
organisation is a multi-level multi-goal system, but they concede that
'the lack of an appropriate description of the structure of an organisation
is a prime reason hindering direct application of analytical and computational methods and techniques to the problems of an organisation'.

THE MANAGEMENT TASK

The control concept, with its fundamental ingredients of standards,
measurement, feedback and corrective action, pervades the whole domain
of management. When the management task is analysed it is found to
consist of the eight major activities shown in Figure 1.5. The first three
activities may be regarded as belonging to the realm of strategy, often
involving the enterprise in long term commitments, but as Figure 1.5
suggests, all the activities of the management process are interconnected
and interdependent. Each has implications on the scope and freedom of
action that is available to the others, and with appropriate feedback, as
shown in Figure 1.5, an opportunity to adapt to changing circumstances is
offered.

In some ways the model described in Figure 1.5 is reminiscent of the
hypothetico-deductive approach to science. This scientific method suggests that in the light of experience the scientist puts forward a hypothesis, which is a model of behaviour of the system that he has been
studying. The hypothesis explains past phenomena and can be used to

depict behaviour under new conditions, in other words for predictive purposes. The hypothesis is then put to the test by conducting an experiment,
the results of which are compared with the prediction. If the experiment
does not refute the prediction, the hypothesis stands and is then used for
further predictions. But if the experimental results fail to conform to the
prediction, the hypothesis must be modified or discarded in favour of a
new hypothesis, and the process is then repeated. This continuous challenge to the hypothesis is the essence of the hypothetico-deductive
method.[19]

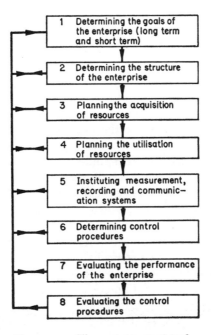

Figure 1.5   The management task

The management task incorporates some interesting analogous ingredients. The planning function is a manifestation of the management's
belief that it has a hypothesis about the behaviour of the system (the
enterprise, a department, a section). In other words, the management
makes some assumptions about the way in which the system behaves and
these assumptions constitute the model, or the hypothesis. The expectations of management as to the reactions of the system to various actions
specified in the plan are in fact a prediction, and the execution of the plan
constitutes an experiment. If the expectations come true, then management is entitled to continue to hold its previous set of beliefs about the

behaviour of the system, but if the expectations do not come true then this set of beliefs becomes suspect and requires a thorough re-examination.

There is perhaps one major point where the analogy between the scientific method and the management process does not hold, namely that in designing an experiment the objective of the scientist is to *refute* the hypothesis in question, whereas the objective of the manager is to *uphold* it. The scientist is free, and indeed encouraged, to go to any length in devising critical experiments to test hypotheses, whereas the manager must always bear in mind that a critical experiment may not only mark the end of his hypothesis, but also the collapse of the enterprise and the end of his career. From the scientist's viewpoint the manager's 'experiments' are, therefore, bound to be somewhat 'conservative' in character.

GOALS AND STRUCTURE

Without predetermined goals, there is no meaning to the management activity. In the absence of goals it is impossible to make any statements about the success or failure of the organisation, or to assess its progress (progress towards what?). Any management decision is then just as good, or just as bad, as any other; indeed how can one judge what is a good decision unless one can ascertain that it is conducive to producing desirable results ('desirable' being defined by the degree to which the predetermined goals can be realised)?

There are, of course, numerous instances when senior managers fail to state explicitly the objective of the enterprise, so much so that Churchman was led to write: 'We don't know what value measures characterize the activities of business firms, that is, we do not know what it is that business is attempting to maximize'.[17] Churchman gave expression to the intense frustration felt by so many management scientists and operational research workers who try to elicit from top management simple answers to the question: 'What are you trying to achieve?' The answers are often vague, inconsistent and sometimes even contradictory.

One stock answer often quoted in the literature, is expressed as a theory of survival: 'The goal of the organisation is to survive'. Profit maximisation, the provision of an efficient product or service, a policy of diversification—all these (so it is argued) are strategies formulated to ensure the attainment of this single goal: survival. These are attractive and compelling arguments, but without specific embellishments the goal of survival cannot generally provide an operational yardstick with which the performance of a system and the quality of its management can be assessed. It may be possible for a firm to survive by adopting one of many alternative strategies, so that if these alternatives are to be compared 'survival' needs to be more explicitly defined (e.g. elimination of competitors, capturing a higher share of the market, introducing new competitive products, etc.).

Many ambiguities which an observer encounters when he tries to identify the goals for an enterprise result from the definition of the organisation structure. By dividing the work between departments a set of goals is automatically generated for each department. It is reasonable to expect a sales department to see its objective as that of maximising sales, or a production department as that of maximising output and reducing unit costs.

Thus, the organisation structure defines systems within systems, each with its own goals and its own procedures. It is only to be expected that many situations may arise in which the goals of subsystems are found to be in conflict, so that for any *given* organisation structure an expression of an overall goal that would accommodate already existing goals of the various subsystems may well lead to the amorphous generalisations that are so often encountered in practice. It is more likely, at least theoretically, to expect a more succinct description of an overall goal *before* the organisation structure is determined, and indeed to expect that the overall goal would be the primary determinant in the design of the structure. In reality, however, these matters never remain static for long. Each subsystem adapts to the environment and develops an identity of its own, its procedures evolve and its goals are then modified under the catalytic effect of changing circumstances. Thus, even if an observer is able to determine clearly the overall goal of an enterprise when it is set up, he is likely to find that after a while the effect of the subsystems becomes substantial enough to invalidate the original definition of the goal and to result in more complex statements about the overall goal that give some expression to the entrenched interests of the subsystems.

THE PLANNING FUNCTION

Planning consists of translating goals into a projected series of activities, the purpose of which is to ensure that the goals can indeed be attained. A useful distinction can be made between strategic planning and tactical planning. The first is concerned with the acquisition or conversion of major resources, the second with the utilisation of these resources. The time scale can be very different for strategic and for tactical planning. The time involved in the construction and installation of plant may be measured in months, even in years, whereas production schedules for operating the plant are often related to time intervals measured in weeks or in days.

Clearly, strategic and tactical planning are closely linked. A decision to acquire a plant cannot be made without some idea as to how the plant will be used. Indeed, the performance characteristics of the plant may be the crucial determinants in the final choice of its design, its size and its flexibility of operation. Similarly, once a decision to build a new plant has been made, very little room may be left for manoeuvre at the tactical planning level. The design characteristics of large installations for continuous processing in the chemical industry or for mass production in the

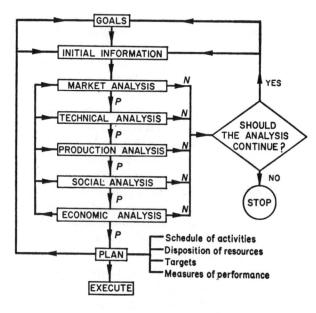

P — result of the analysis is positive
N — result of the analysis is negative

Figure 1.6   Planning

engineering industry are often such that the production rates may not be varied beyond given limits, that certain physical conditions must be strictly maintained, that particular interactions between the plant and human operators must not be violated—and all these constraints imply that the range of alternatives that are open to the production planner can become rather narrow.

The primary elements of the planning process are depicted in Figure 1.6 (see also Bowerman and Littauer[18]). It consists of five types of analyses under the heading marketing, technical, production, social, economic.

.Although these five areas are shown in a given sequence in Figure 1.5, it is not suggested that the analyses need always be carried out in this (or in any other) particular sequence. Also, these areas may vary in importance, depending on the circumstances. In some cases the analysis of the market may be all important, in others the social implications of technical or production solutions may be crucial. Furthermore, in any given situation the relative prominence of, say, economic considerations may be very different for strategic planning than for tactical planning.

The essential feature of Figure 1.6 is, again, feedback. The results of each analysis are fed into the next one, until a plan emerges, and the details of the plan may indicate that further information is required, or that some goals need to be re-examined, until finally a plan ready for execution is presented. The plan consists of a timetable of activities, a schedule for the use of resources, a list of targets and a set of standards of performance.

Some of the analyses in the planning process may yield negative results, in which case more information may be sought, or the goals modified. Of course, if the analyses persist in giving discouraging results in spite of further information (needless to say, the cost involved in collecting data and providing information must also be considered), and if no further changes in the definition of goals can be accommodated, the planning exercise becomes abortive, and this is signified by the circle marked 'stop' in Figure 1.6.

MEASUREMENT AND COMMUNICATION

The vital role of measurement in the management process is clearly shown in Figures 1.3 and 1.4. The purpose of measurement is to generate information about the performance of the system, so that readjustments and modifications to the instructions given to the system can take place whenever required.

This is the crux of the measurement activity—to provide information needed for *action*. To differentiate between information that is not required for action and information that is so required there is a tendency in recent literature to add the word 'management' to the latter: there is thus supposed to be a difference between 'accounting' and 'management accounting', and similarly the term 'management information systems' has become quite popular, although it is difficult to conceive of any formal information system that should justifiably be maintained in an organisation if it is not intended for managerial purposes. In the context of the management process as described in Figure 1.5 we need only be concerned with information that is likely to be relevant to the planning and control functions.

In Figure 1.3 a device called 'recorder' is engaged in measuring a given

characteristic of the output of the system and then a message is transmitted to the controller for evaluation and possible action. A discussion
of the nature of messages in a communication network will be found in a
later chapter, but what it is perhaps pertinent to mention here is that there
are three principal forms of records resulting from the measurement
activity:

> a continuous record
> a record of periodic observations
> a record of random observations

The continuous record is often employed in automatic recording devices:
temperature or pressure graphs traced by a pen recorder, details of
interviews recorded on tape, action recorded on a film (strictly speaking the
cine-camera takes shots at discrete time intervals, but for most practical
purposes a film shot at a normal speed is a continuous record). In industrial and business systems periodic records are very common: production
and sales statistics are given at weekly, monthly, quarterly and/or yearly
basis; accounts and other financial data are often prepared quarterly and
annually. Random observations are used in statistical quality control, in
activity sampling, in traffic counts—to mention just a few examples.

Suppose that the entity that needs to be measured is the level of cash.
The three types of monitoring cash are shown in Figure 1.7. The continuous
record gives complete information about inflows and outflows of discrete
sums, resulting in a step-wise trace as in Figure 1.7(a). In Figure 1.7(b)
an observation is recorded at constant time intervals and in Figure 1.7(c)
at random intervals. When the frequency of periodic or random observations increases, the resulting record will increasingly resemble the continuous record, but unless this frequency is extremely high the impression
that the controller gets about the state of cash in the system may very well
depend on what type of measurement is used.

The information transmitted to the controller need not, of course,
coincide with the available record. With the introduction of computers
there may be a misguided tendency on the part of some systems analysts
to design for transmission of all available information, with the result that
a voluminous printout is dumped on each manager's desk every Monday
morning, leaving him to sift the information on which he should act. It is
more common to expect the transmitter of the information to have certain
guide lines as to what should be transmitted to the manager, so that the
recorded data may go through a filtering device and the information
received by the manager is but a fraction of the available record. Figure
1.8 shows an example of information by exception: suppose that for the
case described in Figure 1.7 the manager wishes to be alerted only when

the cash exceeds L_2 or is under L_1. The resultant truncated record depends on which type of measurement is used as a base. Figure 1.8(a) is taken from Figure 1.7(a) and Figure 1.8(b) and 1.8(c) from 1.7(b) and 1.7(c) respectively. Again the manager's impression of what is happening to the cash

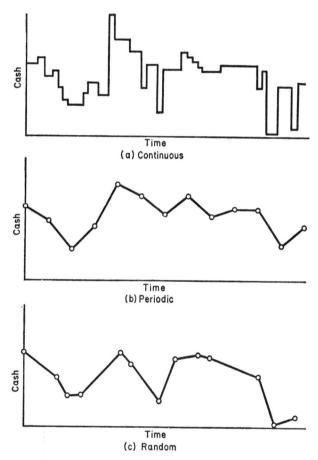

Figure 1.7   Three types of measurement (time triggered)

level in the system depends on the type of measurement employed (and, of course, on the screening levels L_1 and L_2). For example, in Figure 1.8(b) only two warning signals regarding a low cash position are generated, whereas in Figure 1.8(c) there are five such signals for the same time period.

There is also (as we shall see in Chapter 5) a useful distinction between

2*

time triggered and event triggered messages in the communication network. Records such as in Figure 1.7(b) are time triggered: at certain
predetermined points in time observations are recorded and presented.
Information such as in Figure 1.8 is event triggered: each time an event
belonging to a specified class occurs (cash level above L_2 or under L_1) a
signal is transmitted to the manager.

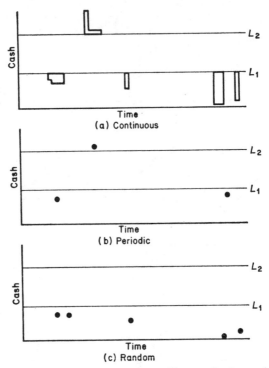

Figure 1.8   Information by exception depending on the type of measurement
(event triggered)

These examples suffice to indicate that measurement and transmission
of information can be carried out in a number of ways and that their
implications for the controller can be far reaching. The design of the
monitoring activity must, therefore, be based on certain hypotheses about
the performance of the system and the kind of action that the controller
needs to take in various circumstances. It is naive to suggest that monitoring can be entirely divorced from the rest of the control function and that
it can be considered in isolation. Not only is it important to ensure that the
characteristics that are selected to be measured are indeed relevant to the

control task, but the type of measurement itself and the mode of information are also a function of this task.

CONTROL, EVALUATION AND DECISION MAKING

In discussing the behaviour of the system in Equation (1), reference was made to the various factors that determine the performance characteristics of the system at any given time. A similar expression may be used to describe the behaviour of the controller of the system:

$$D_n = g(S_n, D_{n-1}, E_n, F_n) \qquad (2)$$

In this expression, the behaviour of the controller, as characterised by his decision D_n in the time interval n, is determined by the prevailing state of the system S_n, by the previous decision D_{n-1}, and by the prevailing values of the endogenous variables E_n and the exogenous variables F_n. From this general description one may point out several possible modes of control:

Open loop—where the control operation is independent of the state of the system and of any feedback information about changes in the system's performance.

Closed loop—where feedback information is vital to the operation of the controller (such as in Figures 1.3 and 1.4).

Adaptive—where the control procedures are purposely designed to allow for a learning process to take place and for the controller to adjust to the environment as, for example, in biological systems.

Industrial systems can rarely employ open-loop control with impunity and in the context of the discussions in this book the term 'control' is therefore used in the sense of a closed-loop process. Also, the controller is identified as a decision maker, whose task is to analyse the information transmitted to him and then to make a decision with the purpose of affecting the future state of the system in a particular way.

What, then, is a decision? And how can one distinguish between different types of decisions? The Shorter Oxford English Dictionary defines decision as 'the action of deciding (a contest, question, etc.), settlement, determination, a conclusion, . . . the making of one's mind'. Clearly, a decision involves a choice of a course of action from several available possibilities. The provision of choice as an essential element in decision making raises the question of how the decision maker ranks the various alternatives and whether he is free to choose between them; this question and allied issues associated with the decision process are discussed in Chapters 7 and 8.

A global classification, which I believe is often useful in the study of decision making, is the distinction between decisions about the products (or services) that the enterprise provides, decisions about the resources that the organisation employs, and decisions about the organisation structure and control procedures. The first category pertains to activities that are directly associated with specifying the products; the second relates to the acquisition or the utilisation of financial, human and material resources; the third category involves decisions about the structure of the enterprise, the formal relationship between departments and individuals, the information and communication systems, and the procedures which need to be followed when decisions in the first category are considered.

This is why in the final stages of the management control process described in Figure 1.5 a distinction is made between evaluation of the performance of the enterprise and evaluation of the control procedures. The first (stage 7 in Figure 1.5) culminates in decisions about the product or about resources ($A1$ and $A2$ respectively in Table 1.1) and the latter (stage 8 in Figure 1.5) in decisions about the organisation structure and the control procedures currently employed in the enterprise ($A3$ in Table 1.1).

TABLE 1.1   Types of decisions

Dimension A Area of application	Dimension B Routine scale	*replica-* *tion*	*fre-* *quency*	Dimension C Relation to the present
1. Products or services ('the aims')	1. (routine)	high	high	1. Do nothing, or maintains the status quo
2. Resources ('the means')	2.	high	low	2. Modify an existing activity
3. Organisation structure, procedures	3.	low	high	3. Stop an activity
	4. (*ad hoc*)	low	low	4. Start an activity

There are four kinds of decisions that a manager can take:
- to do nothing (made explicitly or implicitly)
- to change the intensity level of a given activity or to modify on existing procedure
- to stop an activity/procedure
- to start an activity or a new procedure

Another dimension in a scheme for classifying decisions can be described by *frequency* and *replication*. The frequency with which a given decision has to be made within a given space of time is a measure of the repetitiveness of the task of the decision maker. Replication is to do with the uniformity in the definition of the problems that the decision maker has to face; the greater the variations in these problems the lower the level of replication. Thus, decisions with high replication and high frequency are *routine decisions*, while those with low replication and low frequency may be called *ad hoc* at the other end of a 'routine scale'. The division into 'high' and 'low' levels of frequency and replication is, of course, a matter of judgement based on definition and agreement, but this may be easier to accomplish than to differentiate between routine and *ad hoc* decisions without resorting to questions of frequency and replication.

The action taken by a controller of a system, or indeed any decision, may therefore be characterised by a classification scheme based on three dimensions, as summarised in Table 1.1. This is not intended as a comprehensive classification and there are undoubtedly many other factors that may be brought in, depending on what the classification scheme is to be used for. But even the comparatively crude framework provided in Table 1.1 may help to identify and monitor every single decision that a manager makes, so that if, for example, a manager is found to be engaged in the main in decisions of the type $A1$ $B1$ $C3$ then some interesting information about the role of the manager in the system is thereby obtained.

One important aspect of the control of industrial systems is that all too often the control function is not assigned to a single manager. Even when responsibility for certain tasks is delegated by one manager to another there are various procedures that determine the circumstances in which the former is expected to intervene. The simple process shown in Figure 1.3 provides a crude model for the case of the single controller, but for administrative systems a far more elaborate description is needed to show how other controllers fit into the picture, and this theme is pursued in the following three chapters.

REFERENCES

1. Exodus, 18: 21–23.
2. Adam Smith (1776) *An inquiry into the nature and causes of the wealth of nations*, Book I, Chapter I.
3. Gross, B. M. (1964) *The managing of organizations—the administrative struggle*, Collier–Macmillan, London.
4. *Ibid.*, Chapter 12.
5. Barnard, C. (1948) *The functions of the executive*, Harvard University Press.

6. Simon, H. (1957) *Administrative behavior*, Macmillan, New York, p. 135.
7. Paterson, T. T. (1966) *Management theory*, Business Publications Ltd., Chapters 7–10.
8. *Fortune* (Dec. 1967) p. 113.
9. Follett, M. P. (1948) *Dynamic Administration—the collected papers of Mary Follett*, edited by Metcalf, H. C. and Urwick, L., Pitman, pp. 109, 111, 148.
10. Taylor, F. W. (1911) *Shop management*, Harper, p. 21.
11. Brech, E. F. L. (1953) *Principles and practice of management*, Longmans, p. 39.
12. March, J. G., ed. (1965) *Handbook of organizations*, McNally, Chicago.
13. Vickers, Sir Geoffrey (1967) *Towards a sociology of management*, Chapman and Hall, p. 104.
14. Lee, A. M. (1969) *Systems analysis frameworks*, Macmillan, London.
15. Mesarovic, M. D. (1962) 'On self organizational systems' in Yovits, Jacobs and Goldstein (ed.), *Self organizing systems*, Spartan, pp. 9–36.
16. Mesarovic, M. D., Sanders, J. L. and Sprague, C. F. (1964) 'An axiomatic approach to organizations from a general systems viewpoint' in Cooper, Leavitt and Shelley (ed.), *New perspectives in organization research*, Wiley, pp. 493–512.
17. Churchman, C. W. (1961) *Prediction and optimal decision*, Prentice Hall, Inc., p. 66.
18. Bowerman, E. R. and Littauer, S. B. (1956) 'Operations engineering', *Management Science*, **2**, 4.
19. Eilon, S. (1979) *Aspects of Management*, Pergamon Press, Chapter 29.

2 Correspondence Between a System and its Controllers*

As we have seen in the previous chapter, a controller of a system is an individual or a device that can bring about a change in the mode of operation of one or several constituent elements of the system. The controller achieves this purpose by transmitting a signal to the system with instructions to the effect that certain operating characteristics are no longer desirable and should be abandoned in favour of other characteristics or levels of operation. For example, when a stock controller issues a requisition for replenishment of an item he is generating a signal which intimates that the stock should be changed from its present level to a new level, and the new level is specified or can be inferred from the replenishment order.

For control to be effective, the system must react to the controller's signal. If there is no reaction, the transmitter of the signal has no control function. Furthermore, the reaction of the system must conform to the type of change specified in the signal, otherwise again no control can be exercised. When we sometimes use the graphic expression 'a driver has lost control of his car' or 'a manager has lost control of his department', we visualise a controller who for a time can change and adjust the performance of a given system (a car, a department) by transmitting signals when appropriate, but at some point he loses the ability to do so, his signals go unheeded and the performance of the system diverges from the controller's intention. One reason for the system's failure to react may be traced to the malfunctioning of the communication network, so that either the signal is distorted during the transmission process, or it fails altogether to arrive at its destination. Another reason could lie in the system itself, when it fails or refuses to perceive or respond to the signal when it does arrive; this failure may be due to internal changes or faults which have developed in some components in the system, or it may be due to the emergence of a conflict of interests between the controller and the system.

* This chapter may be omitted at first reading. 35

It is, of course, possible for only partial loss of control to occur: when the system reacts to some of the controller's signals, but not to others.

There are three types of signal that the controller can use to make his intentions known to the system:

- A continuous signal
- A discrete recorded signal
- A discrete unrecorded signal

The *continuous signal* signifies the controller's intentions by its presence. As long as the signal is transmitted a certain reaction of the system is called for, and when the signal ceases the controller expects this reaction to terminate. Traffic lights are an example of a control mechanism with continuous signals. When a driver approaches a road intersection controlled by traffic lights, he looks at the lights in order to find out whether he is expected to drive through or to stop. The continuous signal acts like a label. Whenever the system is in doubt as to what the controller wishes it to do, it merely examines the label. By transmitting a continuous signal, such as an electric current to light a particular lamp, the controller persistently reiterates his instructions for the whole duration of the period for which they pertain. When he wishes to change his instructions, he switches off one signal and switches on another. The absence of a continuous signal may carry with it either the implication of some predetermined instructions, or it may indicate a failure of the control mechanism, depending on which convention is used.

The *discrete signal* is also used with the purpose of changing previous instructions to the system, but the format is quite different from that used by the continuous signal. The *discrete recorded signal* is transmitted once and the import of the signal as well as the time of its transmission (and/or the sequence in which signals of this type are transmitted or received) are recorded. By referring to the record, the system can update the instructions issued by the controller and ascertain which instructions prevail at any given time. Written instructions in administrative systems are discrete recorded signals. When such a signal is generated, the controller triggers off new instructions to the system, but unlike the continuous signal in a traffic-lights mechanism there is no need for him to reiterate his intentions in a continuous stream of identical communiqués. Indeed, if he were to do that, the system would suspect that something had gone wrong in the control procedure. Also, the discrete recorded signal does not provide a readily convenient label in the way that the continuous signal does. Whenever the system wishes to find the latest state of the controller's instructions, it has to refer to the record and the time lag caused thereby is inevitable. For the sake of easy reference, it is, of course, possible for the system to convert the updated state of a series of discrete signals into a continuous signal, thereby reducing or eliminating the time lag which is otherwise involved when the record has to be consulted.

Verbal instructions fall into the category of *discrete unrecorded signals*. The function of such a signal is the same as that of a discrete recorded signal, but in the absence of a visual record the system must either rely on memory or convert the unrecorded signal to a recorded one in order to establish the latest position of the controller at any moment in time. This is an obvious shortcoming of verbal instructions, but they have the advantage that they can be generated at short notice and without the characteristic delays that are often involved in formulating and comprehending long written instructions.

Which mode of transmission is adopted by the controller, is a matter of practical considerations (convenience, cost, reliability, ease of reference, effect on the system's response, etc.), provided both the controller and the system are fully aware of what convention is adopted, so that no disparity between the intentions of the controller and the interpretations by the system can occur. The choice of which type of signal to use is usually determined by the circumstances in which control is to be exercised. For example, it would be difficult and inefficient to control a road intersection by discrete signals (such as 'go' and 'stop') announced by a loudspeaker. A driver arriving on the scene would have to ask the loudspeaker to repeat the instruction, or ask a passerby whether he has heard the latest announcement. Clearly, the response of the driver under such conditions is bound to be very slow, because of the time lag required in establishing what the controller wants him to do. Similarly, very long verbal or written instructions are difficult to transmit by continuous signals, involving perhaps a code with many labels, which would require time to comprehend and interpret.

But apart from the effect of the type of signal on the system's response time there is the effectiveness of the signal itself to consider. The continuous signal has the connotation of a continuous restatement of the position of the controller. The discrete signal, particularly in administrative systems, may lose some of its effectiveness with time. There may develop a feeling among members of the system that perhaps the controller no longer means what is implied by his last signal, if the passage of time or changing circumstances cast doubt on the validity of prevailing instructions. Perhaps, members of the system argue, the controller has failed to examine the new circumstances, perhaps he has lost track of the timing and content of the last signal and is under a misconception as to what the current instructions are. Such situations call for a reiteration on the part of the controller to reassure the system of his constant vigilance. It can be argued that in some ways reiteration of instructions by discrete signals is even more forceful than by a continuous signal, since the latter does not necessarily give a higher level of assurance of the controller's vigilance than a discrete signal. The impatience of drivers at traffic lights often demonstrates how members of a system, which is reliant on continuous signals, are quick to suspect a lack of agility on the part of the controller to take account of changing circumstances.

Yet, whatever the effect of the signal on the system's response time and on its confidence in the controller, the type of signal used is a means to an end. It provides a framework of conventions for instructions to be transmitted and interpreted which let the system know how to behave and react. The distinction between the three types of signals, which relates in the main to different methods of transmission, provides an interesting dimension when the effectiveness of instructions to the system is considered. However, this distinction is not fundamental to the following discussion on correspondence between the system and its controller and although for convenience arguments often refer to one type of signal, they are equally valid for the other types as well.

TYPES OF CORRESPONDENCE

To summarise, a signal transmitted by a controller may be regarded as an announcement that certain instructions about the operating characteristics of the system are superseded by new instructions. If the instructions that the controller wishes to prevail at any one time are defined as a *state*, the signal is a manifestation of the fact that the controller has switched from one state to another. Similarly, a set of the essential characteristics of the operating conditions of the system may be defined as a state, and the purpose of the controller in transmitting his signal is generally to cause the system to abandon one state and assume another.

The various states of the controller form a set called the *controller's set* and the set of states of the system is called the *system's set*. The relationship between the elements of the respective sets (each element being a state) is called *correspondence*. If the controller switches to state s_1, thereby leading the system to switch to state S_1, then S_1 is said to correspond to s_1. When the relationship between all the elements of the respective sets has been established it defines the *type of correspondence* between the two sets. If there is no correspondence between any element in the controller's set and any element in the system's set, there can be no correspondence between the two sets.

Consider the following example in production control: The states of the system are defined by two characteristics, one specifying the rate of production, the other specifying the product mix. If five rates of production and two product mixes are identified, then there are ten states of the system, as shown in Table 2.1, and the system's set may be denoted by the set $R = \{S_1, S_2, \ldots, S_{10}\}$.

TABLE 2.1   Example for a system's set

		Rate of production				
		1	2	3	4	5
Product mix	1	S_1	S_2	S_3	S_4	S_5
	2	S_6	S_7	S_8	S_9	S_{10}

If each of these states corresponds to a state of the controller, and if the controller's set is described by $r = \{s_1, s_2, \ldots, s_{10}\}$, then there is a *one-to-one correspondence* between R and r, leading to *isomorphism* of the two sets. The term isomorphism is borrowed from mathematical group theory: two sets are said to be isomorphic if a *one-to-one* correspondence exists between the respective elements of the two sets, as shown by Example 1 in Table 2.2. Isomorphic correspondence, therefore, implies that the controller's set and the system's set have the same number of states.

TABLE 2.2   Example of complete correspondence

Example 1 Isomorphic		Example 2 Essentially isomorphic		Example 3 Multiple	
Controller	System	Controller	System	Controller	System
s_1	S_1	s_1	S_1	s_1	S_1, S_2
s_2	S_2	s_2, s_3	S_2	s_2	S_3
s_3	S_3	s_4	S_3	s_3	S_4
		s_5	S_4		

In Example 2, Table 2.2, the controller can assume five states, the system only four. The state S_2 of the system corresponds to either s_2 or s_3 of the controller. As there is no way for the system to differentiate between s_2 and s_3 (in either case the system must take the same action), one of these two states may be regarded as redundant. If we were to use a single label for both s_2 and s_3 and cease to identify them as two separate states, we would have a one-to-one correspondence, so that the situation depicted in Example 2 is essentially isomorphic.

Example 3 shows *homomorphism*, or *one-to-many*, or *multiple correspondence*, namely the system has many more states than the controller. When the latter is at s_1 the system may be either at S_1 or at S_2 and there is no way in which the controller can effectively cause the system to select either. All he can do is signify that he does not wish the system to be either at S_3 or S_4, but the choice between S_1 and S_2 is outside his control. The choice may follow a random process, or indeed it may be made by another controller.

All the examples in Table 2.2 have the property of *complete correspondence*, namely every state of the controller corresponds to some state of the system, and *vice versa*, and the distinction between a *one-to-one correspondence* and a *multiple correspondence* is that the former requires every state of the controller to correspond to a *single* state of the system, whereas in the case of multiple correspondence at least one state of the controller refers to two or more states of the system.

For the sake of convenience, our discussion of correspondence is confined to considering a controller associated with a single system. In administrative systems it is more common to find managers, and hence controllers, monitoring and adjusting the performance of several systems, but this does not affect the definitions proposed here for various types of correspondence. If a controller has a set of states r which includes r_1 states to control one system and r_2 to control another, then we simply ignore the single-controller entity but regard the situation as consisting of two controllers, one with the set of states r_1, the other with r_2. It is, of course, quite conceivable that a particular state in r_1 also implies a particular state in r_2, so that the first system cannot be asked to perform at a certain level without committing the second system to a specific state, in which case a correspondence exists between certain elements of r_1 and r_2. Such a correspondence is often found between controllers who are physically independent of each other, and is not a phenomenon confined to the case when the controller is mentally partitioned into several controllers, each handling only one system. Furthermore, while the identification of control tasks in a given situation may not be difficult, the assignment of these tasks to one or several controllers and the definition of each controller entity is sometimes quite arbitrary. The suggestion, therefore, that we consider the controller as a mechanism that looks after no more than one system does not imply any loss of generality in our discussion.

If the system's set consists of n states and if the controller's set has m states, then $m > n$ is possible only if some of the controller's states are redundant (as shown in Example 2 in Table 2.2). If m does not include any redundant states, then $m = n$ implies a one-to-one correspondence, whereas $m < n$ can occur either in complete multiple correspondence (as in Example 3, Table 2.2) or in incomplete correspondence (see Figure 2.1).

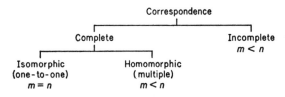

Figure 2.1   Types of correspondence; $m = $ number of non-redundant states of the controller; $n = $ number of states of the system

An example of *incomplete correspondence* is shown in Table 2.3, where one state of the system has no corresponding state of the controller.

TABLE 2.3   Incomplete correspondence

Controller	System
s_1	S_1
s_2	S_2
	S_3

This means that the controller cannot switch to or from S_3. Clearly, the description of the control procedure shown in Table 2.3 must be expanded to explain how the system can ever assume state S_3 (e.g. through the intervention of another controller) or—if the system happens to be in S_3—by what means, or under what circumstances, the controller can assume control.

MULTI-CONTROLLERS

Administrative systems are often controlled by several controllers and a study of the relationships between them can offer a fascinating insight into the workings of the control function.

Table 2.4 shows a system, which can assume one of four states, and two controllers. In Table 2.4(a) two of the system's states are controlled by controller A and two by controller B. All the states of the system are 'accounted for', but from the point of view of either controller the correspondence is incomplete. In such a case, an additional mechanism is clearly needed to effect the transfer of control from one controller to another. In the absence of such a mechanism, the system would be 'locked-in' the subset of states which completely corresponds to one of the controllers, allowing no access to the other controller and therefore no possibility for the system to assume any state outside a given subset.

To avoid this 'locking-in' the controllers must have overlapping states. They can have a partial overlap as in Table 2.4(b), in which both controllers can switch the system to or from S_3, or a complete overlap as in Table 2.4(c), in which the set of states of controller A covers all the states of controller B so that the system appears to have a one-to-one correspondence with controller A but an incomplete correspondence with controller B.

TABLE 2.4   Two controllers

(a) No overlap			(b) Partial overlap			(c) Complete overlap		
Controllers		System	Controllers		System	Controllers		System
A	B		A	B		A	B	
s_1		S_1	s_1		S_1	s_1		S_1
s_2		S_2	s_2		S_2	s_2		S_2
	s_3	S_3	$s_3(A)$	$s_3(B)$	S_3	$s_3(A)$	$s_3(B)$	S_3
	s_4	S_4		s_4	S_4	$s_4(A)$	$s_4(B)$	S_4

When a system is associated with more than one controller, the possibility of conflict must be examined. In Table 2.4(b), for example, what happens if controller A points to s_1 whereas controller B points to s_4? Which controller will the system obey? Such a conflict may even occur in the area of overlap between the controllers, for example in the case of Table 2.4(c) when one controller is at $s_3(A)$ and his fellow controller at $s_4(B)$.

It is, therefore, necessary to specify a hierarchy of control to show how these conflicts are to be resolved. The hierarchical matrices in Table 2.5 refer to the example in Table 2.4(c). A cell in such a matrix refers to the respective states of the two controllers and the entry in the cell indicates which of the two controllers dominates the situation. When both controllers require the system to be at the same state, there is no conflict and the question of dominance does not arise (shown by a dash in the appropriate cells).

In Table 2.5(a) controller A dominates throughout. The only way in which controller B can ensure that he is not overruled is by always agreeing with A. In Table 2.5(b) controller A is usually dominant, but when he points to $s_3(A)$ and B to $s_4(B)$, the latter instruction supersedes the former. Strictly speaking, therefore, a one-to-one correspondence between the system and controller A applies in Table 2.5(a), but not in 2.5(b), since only in the former does the state of the system depend solely on the state of A.

TABLE 2.5   Hierarchical matrices

(a) Controller A dominates			(b) Partial dominance		
		Controller B $s_3(B)$ $s_4(B)$			Controller B $s_3(B)$ $s_4(B)$
	s_1	A A		s_1	A A
Controller	s_2	A A	Controller	s_2	A A
A	$s_3(A)$	$-$ A	A	$s_3(A)$	$-$ B
	$s_4(A)$	A $-$		$s_4(A)$	A $-$

These hierarchical schemes require all the controllers to be constantly alert, to monitor and evaluate unremittingly, to issue instructions without fail. However, there are situations in which a controller chooses to 'switch off' and thereby to delegate for a while the control function to his fellow controllers. This switching off is designated by a *neutral state*, which does

TABLE 2.6   A neutral state

(a) Correspondence				(b) Hierarchical matrix			
Controllers A B		System				Controller B $s_3(B)$ $s_4(B)$ N	
s_1		S_1			s_1	A A A	
s_2		S_2		Controller	s_2	A A A	
$s_3(A)$	$s_3(B)$	S_3		A	$s_3(A)$	$-$ A A	
$s_4(A)$	$s_4(B)$	S_4			$s_4(A)$	A $-$ A	
N					N	B B ?$	
	N						

not correspond to any state of the system. Table 2.6 shows an example, which is similar to that shown in Table 2.4(c), except that each controller also has a neutral state (denoted by N). The hierarchical matrix in Table 2.6(b) gives an illustration of such a scheme. When one controller is neutral, the other is automatically in control. To determine whether one dominates the scene, we ignore for a moment the entries in the last row and in the last column. The rest of the matrix has entries A all over (in the cells where both controllers are in agreement A's instructions can also be said to prevail), so that A in this case is dominant.

TABLE 2.7   Delegation

(a) Correspondence				(b) Hierarchical matrix			
Controllers		*System*			*Controller B*		
A	B			$s_2(B)$	$s_3(B)$	$s_4(B)$	N
s_1		S_1	S_1	A	A	A	A
$s_2(A)$	$\{s_2(B)$ $s_3(B)\}$	S_2	*Controller* $s_2(A)$	B	B	$?$	$?$
$s_4(A)$	$s_4(B)$	S_3	A $s_4(A)$	A	A	—	A
N		S_4	N	B	B	B	$?$
	N						

Table 2.7 shows an example in which A delegates control to B with respect to states S_2 and S_3. When A switches to $s_2(A)$ he expects B to make a choice between S_2 and S_3 and this B must do by pointing either to $s_2(B)$ or to $s_3(B)$, as the other states of B (namely $s_4(B)$ and N) would lead to inconclusive results under these conditions. Notice that although B has several entries in the hierarchical matrix (and not only in the last row) A is effectively dominant here.

The analysis of a system controlled by several controllers leads us to the following conclusions:

1. The controllers' sets must have some overlap if locking of the system in a subset of states (and thereby effectively eliminating one or more controllers from the control function) is to be avoided. When one controller's set has the same number of states as the system's set this overlap is ensured.

2. It is necessary to specify, for example in a hierarchical matrix, how a conflict between controllers is to be resolved.

3. If a controller can assume a neutral state, control passes to the other controllers. However, a controller cannot remain in a neutral state if:
(a) the required state of the system is outside the jurisdiction of the other controllers, or
(b) the other controllers are neutral.
Under either condition the controllers as a group have no control over the system.

4. A controller is said to be dominant if he can always overrule his fellow controllers (except when he is neutral). By definition, therefore, only one overall dominant controller can exist. The relative dominance of the other controllers can be established by considering a hierarchical matrix in which the overall dominant controller is switched to a neutral state. It is possible to devise control schemes with partial dominance, in which overall dominance by any one controller is not possible.

5. Delegation of control by one controller to another can be achieved by the former
(a) switching to a neutral state, provided the conditions in 3 are observed,
(b) having a multiple correspondence with the system.

6. Statements about the correspondence between the system and its controllers and about hierarchical configurations are not sufficient to describe the conditions under which a dominant controller decides to switch to or from a neutral state. Such decisions may be governed not so much by what state the system should, in the view of the controller, switch to, but by the state it is to switch from. In other words they may depend on the switching sequence that is being considered. For example, the switching of the system from state S_1 to S_2 may involve minor costs and the controller may feel justified in leaving the decision to someone else, whereas from S_1 to S_3 may have significant cost implications and the controller would then be unwilling to delegate the decision to others.

RESTRICTED OR IRREVERSIBLE SWITCHING

All the examples in Tables 2.2 to 2.6 make no reference to switching sequences, the implicit assumption being that it is possible for either the controller or the system to switch from any one identifiable state to another. Table 2.8 shows an example of complete correspondence with *restricted switching*. The correspondence is given in (a), and the matrix of possible switching operations is described in (b). The diagonal in this matrix is redundant and a restricted switching is denoted by X. In the example shown in this table the system cannot switch from S_1 to S_2 so that when the controller wishes to switch the system from S_1 to S_2 he must do so through an intermediate state, for example, he may first switch to S_4 and then to S_2. Similarly, switching from S_2 or from S_3 is restricted, while

TABLE 2.8   Complete correspondence with restricted switching

Controller	System
s_1	S_1
s_2	S_2
s_3	S_3
s_4	S_4

From \ To	S_1	S_2	S_3	S_4	
S_1	–	X			
S_2	X	–	X		X denotes prohibited switching
S_3		X	–		
S_4				–	

(a) Correspondence   (b) Switching

switching to or from S_4 is unrestricted. The manual gear in car transmission is a familiar example of restricted switching, where the driver must shift the gear lever through an intermediate state (the neutral position) when changing gears.

Table 2.9 shows an example of *irreversible switching*. It is possible for the controller to switch the system *to* state S_3, but not *from* it. If a situation does arise when the controller switches the system to S_3, he then loses

TABLE 2.9   Complete correspondence with irreversible switching

Controller	System
s_1	S_1
s_2	S_2
s_3	S_3

From \ To	S_1	S_2	S_3
S_1	–		
S_2		–	
S_3	X	X	–

(a) Correspondence   (b) Switching

control. Since it is the controller in this case who causes the system to go to S_3, the correspondence between them is complete, as enumerated in (a). By our earlier definition it is, in fact, a one-to-one correspondence, but with irreversible switching.

Possible switching sequences can be described in network form, as shown in Figures 2.2 to 2.4. Each node represents a state of the system and permitted paths to other states are denoted by arrows. Figure 2.2 shows unrestricted reversible switching, in which the system can move from any one state to another. Figure 2.3 depicts the example in Table 2.8, in which state S_2 is linked with S_4 only, and Figure 2.4 describes the case shown in

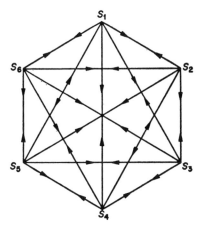

Figure 2.2   Unrestricted reversible
switching

Table 2.9, in which the controller can switch the system to but not from S_3.
The controller's switching may also be restricted, and if the restrictions imposed on the controller do not coincide with those imposed on the sys-

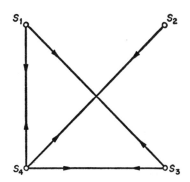

Figure 2.3   Switching network
for Table 2.8

tem, then for each sequence a severer restriction applies. In Table 2.10 an example of a four-state system is given with complete correspondence (s_1 to S_1, s_2 to S_2, etc.); prohibitive switching sequences for the controller and the system are shown in (a) and (b) respectively. The net effect of superimposing (b) on (a) is shown in (c). The network presentation of this example is given in Figure 2.5, where again the resultant network in (c)

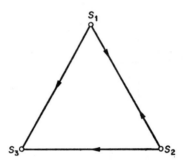

Figure 2.4   Switching network
for Table 2.9

for the controller/system configuration is obtained by considering for each possible link in the network the corresponding links in (a) and (b) and their combined restrictions. On first examination it appears that the controller can assume any of the four states. Certain links in the network are prohibited, but a path does exist to allow the controller to move to any node.

TABLE 2.10   Restricted switching for the controller and the system

(a) Controller switching					(b) System switching				
To	s_1	s_2	s_3	s_4	To	S_1	S_2	S_3	S_4
From					From				
s_1	—	X			S_1	—			
s_2	X	—	X		S_2	X	—		X
s_3			—		S_3	X	X	—	
s_4	X	X		—	S_4		X		—

(c) Controller + system switching

To	1	2	3	4
From				
1	—	X		
2	X	—	X	X
3	X	X	—	
4	X	X		—

Similarly, the system can ostensibly move to any state. But when the two switching networks are combined in (c), we find that the system cannot be switched to or from S_2. Also we find that once it is switched from S_1 either to S_3 or to S_4 it cannot be switched back, so that sooner or later the system will effectively be confined to the two states S_3 and S_4, the others becoming unattainable in the light of prevailing restrictions.

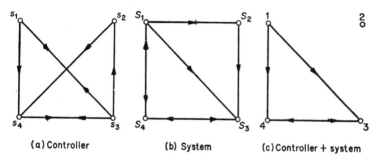

Figure 2.5 Switching network for Table 2.10

Quite clearly, then, when we refer to the constraints which a controller of a system has to contend with, we should not confine our considerations to the controller's switching network. He may be given a freedom of action which could be quite illusory. It is the summation of all the restrictions, those associated with the system as well as those defined for the controller, that describes the effective room for manoeuvre.

PROBABILISTIC CORRESPONDENCE

In all the examples described so far, the correspondence between the states of the controller and the states of the system is of a deterministic nature (state s_1 will lead to S_1 and cannot result in any other state of the system). It is possible, of course, to describe the relationship between the controller and the system in a probability matrix, as in Table 2.11. When the controller turns to state s_1 there is a probability p_{11} that the system will switch to state S_1, a probability p_{12} that it will switch to S_2, and so on. Here there is no one-to-one correspondence between the states of the controller and the states of the system. The level of correspondence and the nature of control become a matter of degree: the higher the probability p_{ij} for state S_j to exist when the controller is at s_i, the higher the level of correspondence between the two; a one-to-one correspondence is obtained when each row and each column in the matrix contains a single unit value, so that all the other probability values are zero, and of course when $m = n$.

In some cases, even the probabilistic model of correspondence between the controller and the system may not be adequate. The matrix in Table 2.11 represents the probability of the system switching to any one state, irrespective of its previous state. But when this probability depends on which transition is to take place, then a matrix similar to Table 2.11 must be presented for *each state* of the system to depict the transition from that

TABLE 2.11   Probability of correspondence between states

		S_1	$S_2 \ldots S_j \ldots S_n$			Total
			States of the system			
States of the controller	s_1	p_{11}	p_{12}			I
	s_2					I
	s_i		p_{ij}			I
	s_m			p_{mn}		I

state to any other state. For example, if Table 2.11 were to be designated 'probability of correspondence—state S_1' then p_{ij} is the probability that the system will undergo a transition from state S_1 to state S_j when the controller switches to s_i. Similarly, when the probability of correspondence depends on the transition of the controller and not on the transition of the system, a comparable set of probability matrices may be presented, each matrix relating to the previous state of the controller.

CONCLUSION

A correspondence between a system and its controllers is an essential feature of the control function. The various types of correspondence highlight certain aspects of the relationships that are involved and contribute to definitions of hierarchy among controllers. The concept of permissible switching sequences adds a useful dimension to the discussion of correspondence and shows how restriction on switching is associated with irreversible transition of a system from one state to another.

Correspondence, switching tables and hierarchical matrices were considered here in static terms to describe certain aspects of control at a given point in time. There is, of course, no reason why these concepts should not be considered dynamically, so that changes with time (for example, in hierarchical relationships) can be monitored and examined.

3 Control Systems with Several Controllers

Any system that has a control mechanism can be relied upon to work satisfactorily as long as the control mechanism does not deteriorate or break down. By 'satisfactorily' I mean that the behaviour of the system and its performance adhere to a set of prespecified standards. Whether this set is an optimal one or can be improved upon with time, is a separate problem. Once the standards are defined and the control mechanism is constructed accordingly, it is expected to react whenever the standards are violated.

Control mechanisms, however, are susceptible to wear and failure, and when they cease to operate, there is a danger that the system will perform below standard. Take, for example, an electric water heater, controlled by a thermostat. If the thermostat fails, the heater will heat the water well above the permissible temperature level. Or consider the housewife who happily leaves her home to the mercy of a fully automated cooker, only to come back and find the fire brigade trying to salvage the furniture. A managerial control system is perhaps even more prone to wear and tear: instructions get ignored or circumvented, procedures misinterpreted or forgotten. And soon an intricate and polished communication and control system is no longer fully effective. How can we guard against this happening?

There are, broadly speaking, three methods that can be used. The first is to employ several identical control mechanisms to operate in concert. The term 'identical' should be interpreted here as meaning that the mechanisms are designed to operate and to react to the same conditions and stimuli. Their internal structure and design need not be the same, but any variations in their behaviour are attributed to chance variations.

The second method is to employ non-identical controllers, namely controllers that react to different sets of stimuli. The purpose of linking identical or non-identical control mechanisms is to provide an opportunity for the controllers to help each other in protecting the system from some specified undesirable breakdowns.

The third method is to check, continuously or from time to time, the performance of the control mechanism in relation to the performance of the system and the circumstances in which the system operates. For example, it may be necessary to test whether a production controller continues to adjust the production level when he should, or it may be necessary to determine whether the stimuli that activate the controller are still adequate to deal with the situation and whether control should be transferred to another controller who is better equipped to react to changes in the system. Such an arrangement that calls for the controller's performance to be under scrutiny may be termed *control of control*.

LINKAGES BETWEEN MULTI-CONTROLLERS

The linking of several identical controllers is called *first-order control* and is characterised by the fact that all the controllers are of equal status and have the same opportunity of affecting the state of the system. This does not happen when non-identical controllers are linked, because by definition the controllers are then designed to react to different stimuli and an equal opportunity for them to react may, therefore, not exist. In some cases the linking of two non-identical controllers may lead to *second-order control*, in which one controller acts most of the time and the other only some of the time, or when the first controller fails.

Three types of control linkages are discussed in this chapter:

control in series
control in parallel
conjoint control

These linkages are significant in the way that controllers affect each other, in the way they can impose—or are prevented from imposing—their will on the system, and in the way they affect the probability of breakdown of the system.

Consider a controller that can assume two states: ON or OFF. The

TABLE 3.1   Types of failure to respond

| | | Controller(s) actual response | |
		ON	OFF
The way con-troller(s) should respond	ON	No failure	Failure 1
	OFF	Failure 2	No failure

ways in which a controller actually responds compared with how he should respond are summarised in Table 3.1. There are two types of failure.

Type 1—failure to switch ON when required
Type 2—failure to switch OFF when required

In considering the effect of the control procedure on the probability of failure it is important to bear the distinction between the two types of failure in mind, since each type may be affected in a different way by the control linkage that is adopted.

Take the example of an electric boiler, the temperature level of which is controlled by two identical thermostats connected in series, as in Figure 3.1(a). If both are in perfect working order and switch ON and OFF at

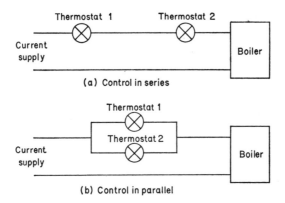

Figure 3.1   Two control linkages

precisely the same temperature levels, the control procedure is just as effective as with one perfect control mechanism. But if one thermostat fails to switch OFF, the electric circuit is broken by the other, and vice versa.

Notice, however, that the performance of the boiler in this case may well depend on the type of failure of the thermostats. As long as this failure occurs in switching OFF, the reaction of one thermostat effectively covers up the sluggishness or complete breakdown of the other. But if both thermostats are at the OFF position and the temperature declines to the point where the current should be switched ON again, and if one

3+

thermostat now fails to react, the system will remain at the OFF position irrespective of what the other thermostat does.

For control to be effective in this case, therefore, it is sufficient for only *one* thermostat to switch OFF but essential that *both* switch ON. Now, if the probability of failure to switch OFF when required is p_0 for each thermostat and p_1 is the probability of failure for each to switch ON, then the operation of the two-thermostat system is described by the following table of probabilities:

TABLE 3.2   Failure of two thermostats

			Thermostat 1			
			Need to switch OFF		Need to switch ON	
			failure	functioning	failure	functioning
			p_0	$1 - p_0$	p_1	$1 - p_1$
	Thermostat 2					
Need to switch OFF	failure	p_0	p_0^2	$p_0(1 - p_0)$		
	functioning	$1 - p_0$	$p_0(1 - p_0)$	$(1 - p_0)^2$		
Need to switch ON	failure	p_1			p_1^2	$p_1(1 - p_1)$
	functioning	$1 - p_1$			$p_1(1 - p_1)$	$(1 - p_1)^2$

The probability that the system is not switched OFF when it should be is

$$P_0 = p_0^2$$

whereas the probability that it is not switched ON consists of:

the probability that thermostat 1 fails when 2 does not $p_1(1 - p_1)$
the probability that thermostat 2 fails when 1 does not $p_1(1 - p_1)$
the probability that both fail p_1^2

i.e. the probability P_1 that the system is not switched ON when it should be is

$$P_1 = p_1^2 + 2p_1(1 - p_1)$$
$$= p_1(2 - p_1)$$

When p_1 is sufficiently small (say, below 0·1), then $(2 - p_1)$ is practically 2 and the probability of failure to switch ON is approximately $2p_1$.

Thus, if a heating system controlled by a single thermostat is compared with a system controlled by two thermostats connected in series (see Figure 3.2), it is evident that the introduction of a second control mechanism provides a good insurance against overheating. However, this is coupled, unfortunately, with an almost doubled chance that the whole system will go out of action and cease to operate altogether. In the case of a water boiler such an outcome may well be justified, but when it is undesirable to have too high a probability for a complete shut-down, the control mechanisms may have to be redesigned with a view to reducing p_1 and it is not difficult to see that if this is done even at the expense of a moderate increase in p_0, the overall effect would generally be beneficial.*

This result applies to any system in which flow is controlled by mechanisms coupled in series. If these mechanisms are valves which adjust the rate of flow of a liquid (the adjustment being to any level up or down the scale, and not necessarily restricted to ON–OFF positions as in the thermostat), then the governing factor is always that valve that allows the lowest rate. Failure to decrease the flow is p_0^n for n valves, and failure to increase it is $1 - (1 - p_1)^n$; and when p_1 and n are sufficiently small this expression is approximately equivalent to np_1.†

The administrative analogy to the control system described above is a chain of executives, who function in sequence with relation to any set of operations which they are supposed to control. Consider the case where an expenditure needs the authorisation of two executives, both equal in stature and each unaffected by the behaviour of the other. Control in series is obtained when authorisation for the expenditure is conditional on *both* executives affirming their signatures on a requisition form (i.e. both must be at the ON position), while only *one* needs to object to stop the expenditure (this executive being at the OFF position). The same procedure applies with a cheque which requires two signatures: it can be cashed when the two signatures are ON; it is worthless if any one signature is OFF.

Here is another interesting administrative situation: a flow of progress

---

* If, for example, p_1 can be halved while p_0 is doubled, the failure to switch ON will have about the same probability for the single controller and the double controller systems. The failure to switch OFF, however, will be p_0 for the single controller and $(2p_0)^2$ for the double controller, the latter probability being the smaller, provided $p_0 < 0.25$.

† $1 - (1 - p_1)^n$

$$= np_1 - \frac{1}{2}n(n-1)p_1^2 + \frac{1}{3!}n(n-1)(n-2)p_1^3 - \cdots - (-1)^n p_1^n$$

The effect of n on the relative values of the second and third terms is shown in the following table

	$\dfrac{\text{second term}}{\text{first term}}$ $= -\frac{1}{2}(n-1)p_1$	$\dfrac{\text{third term}}{\text{first term}}$ $= \frac{1}{6}(n-1)(n-2)p_1^2$
$n = 2$	$-\frac{1}{2}p_1$	0
$n = 3$	$-p_1$	$\frac{1}{3}p_1^2$
$n = 4$	$-\frac{3}{2}p_1$	p_1^2
$n = 5$	$-2p_1$	$2p_1^2$
$n = 10$	$-4.5p_1$	$12p_1^2$
$n = 20$	$-9.5p_1$	$57p_1^2$

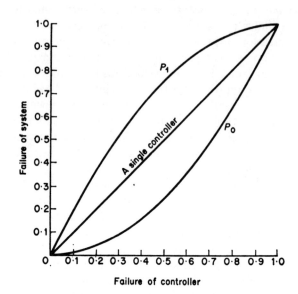

Figure 3.2   Failure of system to switch OFF (P_0) or ON (P_1)
for two controllers in series

reports is subjected to the scrutiny of several executives. Each executive may pick on an item in the reports and start an inquiry or issue instructions for modifications, or stop production. He can be said to be acting in an analogous manner to the thermostat that switches the circuit off. It requires all the executives to acquiesce, or to raise no questions (or not to read the reports) for no action to be taken, and this is when the executives are said to be at the ON position. Notice, however, the significant difference between this situation and the case of the cheque: here ON is indicated by the *absence of reaction* on the part of the executive whereas with the cheque ON requires his *active response*.

Using the multi-thermostat analogy I propose the following definition for the administrative system. In a system in which control is exercised by the intensity of a signal or by two types of action, several control mechanisms are said to be operating in series if one action is triggered off by at least one mechanism, but the other action is enforced by all the mechanisms, and these actions of the mechanisms may be called OFF and ON respectively. The terms ON and OFF are used for convenience; they need not literally have the connotation of switching operations. In the adjustment of, say, a production level, these activities may well relate to pushing the level upwards or downwards, but by the above definition 'upward' is ON only if all control mechanisms are in agreement. If a procedure

is set up whereby an increase in production rate is effected by one controller only, and a decrease by all controllers, then the former is equivalent to
OFF, and the latter to ON.

CONTROLLERS IN PARALLEL

When controllers are connected in parallel, each can 'activate' the system on his own. In contrast to a linkage in series, where all the controllers
need to be ON for the system to be ON but only one controller needs to be
OFF for the system to be OFF, a linkage in parallel requires only one
controller to be ON for the system to be ON but all the controllers have to
be OFF for the system to be OFF. Switches in electrical circuits are a
familiar example of controllers that can be wired in series or in parallel,
and the type of linkage that is adopted has the implications that have
just been described as to whether unanimity of agreement between the
controllers is required for the system to change its mode of activity.

Take the case of a water boiler controlled by two identical thermostats
connected in parallel as in Figure 3.1(b). If the probability of failure of
either thermostat to switch OFF when it should is p_0 and its failure to
switch on is p_1 then the probability of failure of both is as given in
Table 3.1. But now, as both thermostats have to act to switch the boiler
OFF, the probability of failure for the system to switch OFF is

$$P_0 = p_0(2 - p_0)$$

whereas the probability of failure to switch ON is

$$P_1 = p_1^2$$

TABLE 3.3   Summary of probability of failure

	Type 1 (Failure to switch ON) P_1	Type 2 (Failure to switch OFF) P_0
A single controller	p_1	p_0
Two controllers in series	$p_1(2 - p_1)$	p_0^2
Two controllers in parallel	p_1^2	$p_0(2 - p_0)$

The position is, therefore, reversed (see Table 3.3). If in Figure 3.2 the
graphs labelled P_0 and P_1 are relabelled P_1 and P_0 respectively then the
probability of failure for the linkage in parallel is obtained. Clearly, control
in parallel achieves the opposite effect to control in series, namely it
provides a better protection from failure to switch ON (compared with
the single controller), but a poorer protection from failure to switch OFF.

Thus the choice between the two control procedures may depend on the type of failure which is considered to be the least serious.

The following are some examples.

1. In authorising payment (or expenditure), if two executives are assigned to handle the relevant documents and if it is thought that each should be allowed to authorise payment on his own, then the two executives are linked in parallel. When it is necessary to ensure a closer scrutiny of the documents (particularly when large sums of money are involved) and to reduce the risk of authorisation being made when it should not, then a procedure can be adopted which requires *both* executives to agree to the expenditure; the executives are then linked in series. However, as we have already seen, the improved level of protection achieved in this way is coupled with the increased risk that the managers will be over cautious and will fail to authorise expenditure when it is in fact justified.

2. Transactions at counters (e.g. payment of bills, purchase of merchandise), where the volume of business necessitates several counters, are often organised as control in parallel. A transaction is offered by a customer to the controller manning the counter and if the controller approves, the transaction goes through; if he is linked in parallel to the other controllers manning other counters, he need not consult any of them before making his decision. If the customer is dissatisfied with the decision, he can try another counter. This is a familiar sight with vending machines, which are linked in parallel; if a machine rejects a coin, for example, the customer is often seen trying another machine, which sometimes—in fact—accepts the coin. It is only when all the controllers that are connected in parallel reject the customer that the transaction does not take place. The implication in choosing this type of control for counters (and for vending machines) is that the penalty for a failure of Type 2 (see Table 3.1) is not so large compared with need to provide prompt service. Therefore the increased risk of incurring failures of Type 2 by introducing contol in parallel can be tolerated.

3. Components coming off a production line often require inspection. If the volume of production is large and if the utility of a component is not excessive (for example, its monetary value, or its future function), inspection is often carried out by inspectors linked in parallel. As in the previous example, each inspector can 'pass' the components; but if a component fails to pass one inspector, it can be sent to another (or even back to the same inspector) and there is, of course, a chance that it will pass the second time. Operators on the

shop floor and inspectors are fully aware of the fact that such a procedure increases the probability of components passing through when perhaps they should not, but in most cases the alternative of resorting to control in series is thought to be too costly and time consuming.

CONJOINT CONTROL

When control mechanisms are linked in series, it is sufficient for one to be at the OFF position for all the other controllers to be neutralised. This is reminiscent of the power of veto. Members of a committee who have this power may be said to act as controllers in series, and any one member can prevent the others from taking action.

To enable each controller to activate the system without the acquiescence of the others, controllers have to be connected in parallel, as described earlier, but an activity cannot then be stopped unless all the controllers agree to do so. Both control procedures—in series and in parallel—therefore require the collaboration of controllers in one form or another.

There is one mode of control that allows each controller to act on his own, irrespective of whether an activity needs to be initiated or stopped. This control linkage may be called *assertive controllers in parallel*, or better still *conjoint controllers*. In this type of control whenever one controller acts, it is as if the other automatically acquiesce with his decision and all the controllers then act together as a single body.

A lighting circuit for a staircase with two switches illustrates a system with two conjoint controllers: each switch can switch the light on or off on its own, irrespective of the state of the other switch. It is no longer necessary for both switches to act for the light to be on, and in fact we may regard each switch as automatically activating the other; when one goes on it overrides the other, and vice versa.

The advantage of such a procedure is obvious: the system can continue to operate even if one of the controllers breaks down. Unlike the system with several controllers in series or in parallel, which continues to operate for one type of breakdown but fails when another type of breakdown occurs, the functioning of a system with conjoint controllers is assured, as long as at least one controller is operational.

It is important to stress that the distinction between the three types of control linkages discussed here is not solely in the way information flows in the system, but also by the way controllers can affect each other. In administrative systems information flow (of documents or data) may be directed from one executive's tray to another. This implies that there is a delay between the times at which executives make their decisions and that controllers further along the line may well be aware of how previous controllers have acted, or have failed to act, in given situations. This type of information flow requires the controllers to act *in sequence*, and the significance of such a mode of control is discussed further in Chapter 4.

The other form of information flow is that in which data are presented to the various controllers simultaneously, or at least that when a controller is faced with the problem of making a decision, he does so without any prior knowledge of the decisions made by his fellow controllers. Thus, even if the information is not presented to all of them simultaneously, and even if the decisions are not made precisely at the same moment, the fact that each controller makes his decision on his own (he may speculate as to how the others have or will react, but he does not know for sure) means that this case may be treated as if controllers make their decisions *simultaneously*.

An important distinction between the three control procedures in the case of simultaneous decisions is that with linkages in series, or in parallel, each controller acts on the system but not on the other controllers, whereas in conjoint control each controller's actions automatically lead the others to acquiesce. In the first two, disagreement between controllers or failure of one can cause the system to get out of control (e.g. shut down); in the third, disagreement manifests itself in the fact that each controller can always have the last word.

There is one feature common to the three control procedures: that controllers have equal status. Each can affect the other in precisely the same way, although one can prove to be more of a nuisance to the others in the way that he acts or fails to act when he should. Even in conjoint control, where any one controller can overrule the others, his action holds only as long as the others agree with him, otherwise the effect of his decision can be annulled by a counter decision by another controller. With conjoint control, the power of veto is not vested in the individual controllers, as is the case with control in series or in parallel. The power that each controller has to affect the state of the system and the limitations that his fellow controllers can impose on him are very different in the various control procedures; nevertheless, when decisions are made simultaneously, all the controllers have an equal opportunity to affect the outcome and it is in this sense that we regard them as being of equal status.

SECOND-ORDER CONTROLLERS

So far we have been concerned with the coupling of essentially identical control mechanisms, that is mechanisms that are designed to react to the same stimuli. The purpose of having more than one controller, as we have seen, is to provide a better level of protection against some kind of breakdown.

Another way to achieve this objective is by linking non-identical control mechanisms that are designed to react to different feedback signals regarding the performance of the system. In this way, two controllers can be set to respond with different frequencies, one having the function of looking after the system most of the time, and the other being required to step in only occasionally, as and when the need arises. This characteristic of the control procedure is called *second-order control*; the first controller is in a first line of defence, so to speak, and the second controller is kept in reserve.

The main difference, therefore, between first-order or second-order controllers lies in the *frequency* with which the second mechanism needs to operate. If a mechanism is known to deteriorate the more it is activated, owing perhaps to wear of its component parts, then the second-order procedure may have distinct merits. If, however, both mechanisms deteriorate with time, then the first-order arrangement has the advantage that it provides a better control (say of a temperature level within closer limits) without its time dependent reliability being impaired.

It should be pointed out that the type of failure of any one mechanism is just as important in a second-order arrangement as it is in a first-order one. In other words, control can continue to be exercised when one mechanism fails to switch OFF; if either remains at the OFF position and fails to switch ON, the whole system is put out of action. The probabilities for failure of the system as given in Table 3.3 are, therefore, equally applicable to a second-order control system.

Second-order control in series

Take again the example of the water boiler. If two identical thermostats are linked to control the temperature of the water, both are expected to react at the same time, but if we couple two thermostats in such a way that one is set to react at two given temperature levels and the other is set at more liberal levels (i.e. the range between the two levels of the latter includes the two levels of the former), then the second thermostat is only called upon to react when the first fails. In this way a second-order control is established.

Second-order control for two thermostats linked in series is illustrated in Figure 3.3. Thermostat 1 is designed to switch OFF at a temperature level L_1 and to switch ON at l_1, while thermostat 2 is designed to react similarly at L_2 and l_2 respectively.

3*

In Figure 3.3 the relationship between these control levels for (a) and (b) is:

$$L_2 > L_1 > l_1 > l_2$$

In case (a) thermostat 1 is master of the situation for a time, during which thermostat 2 is switched ON. Then at one point thermostat 1 fails to switch OFF when the temperature reaches L_1, so that when it reaches L_2 thermostat 2 intervenes, and as long as thermostat 1 is out of action, thermostat 2

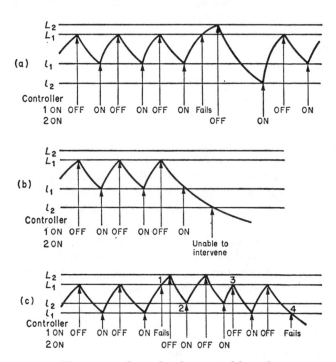

Figure 3.3   Second-order control in series

acts as a first-line controller, except that the temperature now fluctuates between l_2 and L_2, rather than between l_1 and L_1 as before. Subsequently, we see that thermostat 1 is back in action and reacts at L_1 and thermostat 2 becomes passive until its services are required again.

But it very much depends on what kind of failure thermostat 1 is subjected to. In case (a) it fails to switch OFF and thereby it allows thermostat 2 to take over. In case (b), however, it fails at one stage to switch ON and when the temperature eventually falls to l_2 there is nothing that thermostat 2 can do to save the situation, since thermostat 2 is ON in any

case and the linkage in series requires both to be ON for an electric current
to flow to the boiler.

In case (c) the control levels are arranged as

$$L_2 > L_1 > l_2 > l_1$$

that is, the ranges overlap, but the control procedure remains unaffected.
Thermostat 1 acts as a first-line controller for a while and the temperature
fluctuates between l_1 and L_1. At point 1 thermostat 1 fails to switch OFF
and thermostat 2 takes over and switches OFF at L_2. When the temperature decreases to l_2 thermostat 2 (point 2) switches ON and continues to
act as long as thermostat 1 is out of action, with the temperature now
fluctuating between l_2 and L_2. At point 3 thermostat 1 is again operational
and resumes its role as a first-line controller, but when it fails to switch
ON at point 4 thermostat 2 is unable to intervene and the temperature
continues to decrease below the desirable limit. There is, then, essentially
no difference between the case where the control levels do not overlap, as
in (a) and (b), and the case (c) where they do.

Second-order control in parallel

The effect of linking the two thermostats in parallel is shown in Figure
3.4. The case

$$L_2 > L_1 > l_1 > l_2$$

is shown in (a) and (b). In (a) the first-order thermostat is in operation,
while the other thermostat is OFF. Then at one point the first-order
controller fails to switch ON and when the temperature declines to l_2 the
second thermostat is activated. As with a linkage in series, the temperature
fluctuates between l_1 and L_1 when the first-order thermostat is in control
and between l_2 and L_2 when the second-order thermostat takes over.

In (c) the control levels are

$$L_1 > L_2 > l_1 > l_2$$

and, again, as long as controller 1 is operational, the temperature fluctuates
between l_1 and L_1, but when controller 2 steps in the fluctuations are
between l_2 and L_2.

The difference between the linkage in series and the linkage in parallel
lies—as we have already seen—in the type of failure of the first-order
controller that results in the whole system getting out of control.
With the series linkage the system can tolerate the first-order controller
failing to switch OFF, but it shuts down if this controller fails to switch
ON, as shown in Figure 3.3(b). With the parallel linkage the position is
reversed: a failure of the first-order controller to switch OFF can be

tolerated, but if it fails to switch ON, the second-order controller is power-less to intervene.

Clearly, then, if a linkage in series is adopted, it is necessary to mini-mise the risk of the first-order controller committing a failure of type I (see Table 3.1). This can be achieved by designing the controller such that its p_1 (= probability of failure to switch ON when necessary) is low.

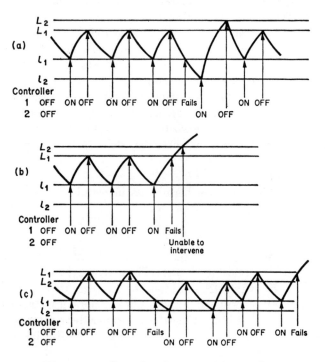

Figure 3.4   Second-order control in parallel

Alternatively, by coupling two (or more) controllers in *parallel* to act to-gether as a first-order controller, the probability of failure to switch ON is drastically reduced (see Table 3.3) and when this parallel linkage is con-nected to a second-controller in series, the risk of a complete breakdown, such as in Figure 3.3(b), is thereby reduced.

Similarly, if a first-order and a second-order controller are linked in parallel, it is desirable to avoid a situation such as that in Figure 3.4(b), and this can be achieved by replacing the single first-order controller by two (or more) identical controls linked in *series*.

Conjoint control

The operation of two non-identical thermostat controllers linked in conjoint control is shown in Figure 3.5. In case (a)

$$L_2 > L_1 > l_1 > l_2$$

and the temperature fluctuates between l_1 and L_1 as long as the first-order controller does not fail to act. When it does, the second-order controller steps in and the temperature fluctuations then depend on the type of failure of the first-order mechanism. If it fails to switch OFF, the control

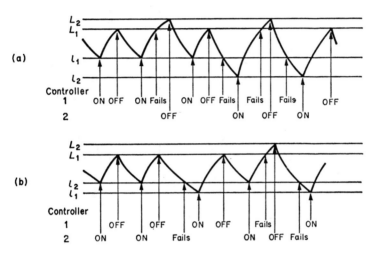

Figure 3.5   Conjoint control

limits become effectively l_1 and L_2; and if it breaks down completely, the control limits become l_2 and L_2. The failure of the whole system depends solely on the failure of the second-order controller, and in this respect conjoint control differs fundamentally from the examples shown in Figures 3.3 and 3.4.

Another way in which first-order and second-order conjoint controllers operate may be illustrated by two pairs of sieves through which beads of varying sizes are processed (the beads are analogous here to signals about the performance of the system). The first-order controller is represented by one pair of sieves: one sieve imposes the lower limit and rejects the beads that are too small; those that do not pass through this sieve are processed through another, which sets the upper limit and does not allow too large beads to pass. Now, if the second-order controller is represented by another pair of sieves, one with holes smaller than the corresponding lower-limit sieve of the first-order and one with holes larger than the corresponding larger-limit sieve, the second pair will not eliminate any beads at all, if the first pair functions properly. But if the first-order controller fails, or is removed, the second pair of sieves will operate as if they were a first-order controller. Only the size of beads that are passed will fluctuate more widely than when the first original pair of sieves is employed.

In Figure 3.5(b) the control limits are such that

$$L_2 > L_1 > l_2 > l_1$$

Here, in the absence of failure, controller 1 acts whenever the temperature reaches L_1 and controller 2 acts when it declines to l_2. Thus, the control function is shared by the two controllers: one guards against overheating, the other against overcooling.

In this case, neither controller is a first-order controller throughout, although each performs a function that is attributable to a first-order controller. Similarly, neither is a second-order controller throughout, although each can step in when the other fails. This mode of control may be called *hybrid control*.

Conjoint control may, therefore, take three forms:

1. *First order*—all controllers are essentially identical with respect to the stimuli to which they react.
2. *Second order* (or higher)—a controller is said to be second order when reacting to levels of performance of the system which lie outside the levels that trigger off the first-order controller. In other words the second-order controller takes over whenever the first-order controller fails.
3. *Hybrid*—each controller performs some functions of first-order and some of second-order control.

Further comments

The definitions of first-order and second-order control lead to the following conclusions.

1. Two controllers acting on double action limits (such as in Figures 3.3, 3.4, 3.5) are equal if $L_1 = L_2$ and $l_1 = l_2$, and the controllers are then first-order.
2. If a second-order controller is identified in a system there must be at least one first-order controller. If the latter breaks down, or is removed from the system altogether, the second-order controller steps in and takes over the function of the first-order controller.
3. If two controllers are linked in series or in parallel the risk of certain failures in the control function is greatly reduced compared with the

single controller system, but the risk of a complete failure of the system is increased (Table 3.3). If one of the controllers acts as a second-order controller then this risk of a complete breakdown can be greatly diminished when the first-order controller is replaced by two or more identical controllers linked in an appropriate way.

4. Hybrid control is a particular feature that can be built into conjoint control, but not into control in series or control in parallel.

5. Hybrid control can cause the system to be very tightly controlled and in administrative systems this can lead to acute frustration for the controllers and for the controlled.

HIERARCHICAL CONTROL

Hierarchy in an organisation is often identified as the authority vested in one management level to intervene and overrule decisions made at another level. As we have seen, even in pure series and parallel linkages of first-order control each controller has some power over his fellow controllers, in the sense that he can—under certain circumstances—prevent the others from acting. It is, therefore, useful to define a hierarchical relationship between two controllers as one that allows one controller to override another, but not *vice versa*. In other words, we draw a distinction between the case where the overruling procedure is mutual for the two controllers (as in first-order control) and the case where it is one sided.

In this respect second-order control does demonstrate some facets of hierarchical relationships; they are manifest by the fact that a second-order controller *need not act as frequently* as a first-order controller. The second-order controller need not even monitor continuously the performance characteristics of the system or all the decisions of the first-order controller, arrangements can be made only for certain cases to be referred to the second-order controller.

Second-order control in series or in parallel gives the first-order controller the power to lead the system to a state beyond the control of the second-order controller. The power of intervention of the second-order controller is therefore limited, as shown in the examples in Figures 3.3 and 3.4. On the other hand, the second-order conjoint control allows the second-order controller to intervene *whenever* the first-order controller fails.

Another way in which hierarchical control can be designed is for control to be *transferred* from one controller to another, when certain symptoms in the operating characteristics of the system become apparent. The procedure for general practitioners to refer patients to specialists or to hospitals is one such example. Here the decision to transfer the patient lies with the general practitioner. In other words the controller is responsible for identifying the circumstances under which he brings another controller into the picture. In other cases the decision to transfer control may rest with a separate controller.

4 Control of a Two-State System

THE TWO-STATE SYSTEM

The smallest number of states that a controller or a system can assume is two, since by definition a single-state system cannot be controlled and similarly a single-state 'controller' can have no effect on the system. There are numerous examples of systems operating in a two-state mode: lighting circuits (the light is either ON or OFF), appointments by selection boards (a candidate is either accepted or rejected), and so on. The digital computer, which conforms to the rules of binary logic, is another such example. For the sake of convenience let us label the two states as 1 and 0, or ON and OFF respectively. There is no special merit in these names, except that 1 and 0 are used in binary arithmetic and ON and OFF describe the two states of a current flowing through electrical circuits. As the two-state operation is fundamental to the understanding of the control function, we shall now examine the two-state control process in some detail.

THE TWO-STATE SINGLE CONTROLLER

If the controller may be either in the state ON or in the state OFF, and similarly if the system may assume either of these states, then all the possible control procedures may be listed in what is generally called a 'truth table' (see Table 4.1). Each procedure expresses the correspondence between the states of the controller and the states of the system. For example, in procedure 2 when the controller switches to ON, the system

TABLE 4.1 Four procedures for a two-state single controller

Controller	Procedure	System			
		1	2	3	4
ON		ON	ON	OFF	OFF
OFF		ON	OFF	ON	OFF

moves to state ON, and when the controller switches to OFF, the system reverts to OFF.

Of the four possible procedures, the first and last have no need for a controller since in neither case does the state of the controller affect the state of the system. Procedure 2 calls for *affirmation* because it requires the system to assume the state indicated by the controller. Procedure 3 is that of *negation* (or *inversion*), and here the state of the system is the opposite of that of the controller. If, in procedure 3, the labels of the states of the system are reversed and the labels of the state of the controller are left as they are, then procedure 2 is obtained. This is reminiscent of the NOT operator in Boolean algebra and the NOT gate in circuit theory: when an output is connected to an input through a NOT gate, the output is ON when the input is OFF and *vice versa*.

We see, therefore, that for a two-state system with a single controller A, only two control procedures are feasible.

Procedure	Controller	System
Affirmation	A	As A (or A for short)
Negation	A	Not A (or $\bar{A}$ for short)

In administrative systems the NOT gate has the connotation of management by exception. The controller may be described as a passive component in the system; as long as he remains in a state of passivity (denoted as OFF) the activity under his charge continues unabated. When he perceives an exception to normal working, he takes action (i.e. he switches to the ON position) causing the system to stop. This is precisely how a NOT gate is defined.

LINKAGES BETWEEN SEVERAL CONTROLLERS

Suppose that several controllers are assigned to the same system, so that there is complete correspondence between the states of each controller and the states of the system. It is important to note that under such conditions it is not the state of the individual controller that necessarily determines the state of the system. If that were the case, then a one-to-one correspondence would have to exist, which means that either the roles of the controller are incompatible (when one controller requires it to be in a different state), or the controllers must all act in unison to ensure that no conflict occurs. When the controllers are set to work in unison then a one-to-one correspondence exists not just between the system and each controller, but between all the controllers as well.

In the absence of a one-to-one correspondence, the state of the system is determined by the combination of the states of the controllers. The way in which the controllers are connected then defines the control procedure for the system, namely the correspondence between the composite state of the group of controllers as a whole and the state of the system.

TIME-INDEPENDENT GATES[1,2]

The concepts of AND gates and OR gates, which are used in designing electrical circuits, are helpful in considering the fundamental ways in which controllers can be connected to form control procedures. To these concepts we add the ANDOR gate, which can be constructed as a combination of the basic AND, OR the NOT gates, as we shall see later. The ANDOR gate is not commonly identified as a separate gate in circuit theory, but it is a convenient concept to employ, particularly in the study of administrative control procedures. The three gates (henceforth, the terms *gate* and *link* are used interchangeably) are defined as follows:

AND gate—if there are several inputs connected to an output through an AND gate, the output is ON when all the inputs are ON and the output is OFF when one or more inputs are OFF.

OR gate—if there are several inputs connected to an output through an OR gate, the output is ON when one or more inputs are ON and the output is OFF when all the inputs are OFF.

ANDOR gate—if there are several inputs connected to an output through an ANDOR gate, each input can cause the output to be switched ON or OFF.

To these (see also Figure 4.1) we should add the NOT gate, which was discussed earlier. It does not define any linkage between controllers, but acts as a negation operator:

NOT gate—if an output is connected to an input through a NOT gate, the output is ON when the input is OFF and *vice versa*.

The operation of the AND, OR and ANDOR gates is summarised in Table 4.2(a) which shows the state of a system with two controllers A and B, where each controller has two states designated as 1 and 0 (or: ON and OFF, or: TRUE and FALSE) respectively. These results are summarised in a form of truth table in Table 4.2(b), in which four composite states for the two controllers are listed (one state when both are ON, two states when one is ON and one is OFF, and one state when both are OFF).

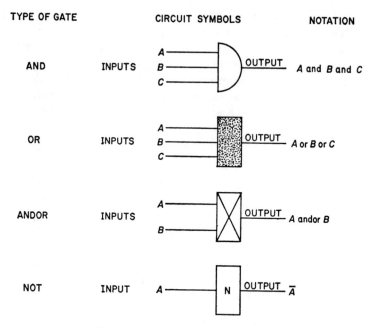

TYPE OF GATE　　　　　CIRCUIT SYMBOLS　　　　　NOTATION

Figure 4.1　Four types of gates

Changing the state of the system

The results in Table 4.2 reveal some interesting facets of the way in which each controller can effect a change in the state of the system. Suppose that the system is in state I and that the two controllers are linked by AND. If an event occurs which causes either controller to want to change the state of the system from I to 0, he is able to effect such a change.

TABLE 4.2(a)　State of system for given states of its two controllers A and B

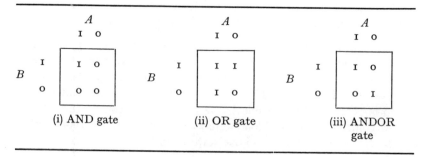

(i) AND gate　　　　　(ii) OR gate　　　　　(iii) ANDOR gate

TABLE 4.2(b) The two-state two controller system
(summary of Table 4.2(a))

Controllers		System		
A	B	AND	OR	ANDOR
I	I	I	I	I
I	O	O	I	O
O	I	O	I	O
O	O	O	O	I

And if both controllers want the system to change, then again the control procedure AND allows both to act and to achieve that aim.

If, on the other hand, the system is in state o, then the action of one controller, or even of both, may not be effective in changing the state of the system from o to I when the controllers are linked by AND. It all depends on the initial state of the controllers. For example, if one is at I and the other at o then only the latter can effect a change in the state of the system, and if the former acts (by changing his state), or if both act simultaneously (each reversing his own state), no change in the state of the system will result.

In the case of the OR link the situation with regard to change is a mirror image of AND: if the system is at o either controller, or both, can effect a change; if the system is at I then the result depends on the initial state of the controllers (see Table 4.3).

TABLE 4.3 One or two controllers acting to
change the state of the system

System's initial state	Controllers' action	Effect on the system		
		AND	OR	ANDOR
I	one acts	change	?	change
	both act	change	?	no change
O	one acts	?	change	change
	both act	?	change	no change

Notes:
1. A controller acts by switching his initial state (from I to o or from o to I).
2. The symbol ? in the table means that the effect on the state of the system depends on the initial state of the controllers.

The ANDOR link allows either controller to trigger off a change, but if both controllers act simultaneously (each reversing his own state) then no change in the state of the system can take place, and this result holds irrespective of the initial state of the system or of the controllers.

The NOT gate

The combination of these three gates with a NOT gate causes the system to behave in the opposite way to that described in Table 4.3, and the control procedures which then result are:

$$NAND = NOT \ AND$$
$$NOR = NOT \ OR$$
$$NANDOR = NOT \ ANDOR$$

The contrast between the AND and the NAND procedures is shown in Table 4.4 and similar relationships between the controllers and the system for NOR and for NANDOR are also given in the table.

TABLE 4.4   NAND, NOR, NANDOR

Controllers		System					
A	B	AND	NAND	OR	NOR	ANDOR	NANDOR
I	I	I	O	I	O	I	O
I	O	O	I	I	O	O	I
O	I	O	I	I	O	O	I
O	O	O	I	O	I	I	O

It is not difficult now to see how ANDOR can be described in terms of AND, OR and NOT. If an AND procedure and a NOR procedure are linked by an OR operation, the ANDOR procedure is obtained, hence

$$ANDOR = (AND) \ OR \ (NOR)$$

similarly

$$NANDOR = (NAND) \ AND \ (OR)$$

Examples

Several examples of electrical circuits are shown in Figure 4.2. The three switches in (a) control the current flowing through the line; they are connected in series and form an AND gate. The switches in (b) are in parallel and form an OR gate. In (c) the output is ON if either A and B are ON or if C is ON, while (d) shows an example where A and either B or C should be ON for the output to be ON. In (e), when the solenoid C is energised it moves the switch to an OFF position, and when the solenoid is not energised the switch moves to an ON position: the output for the

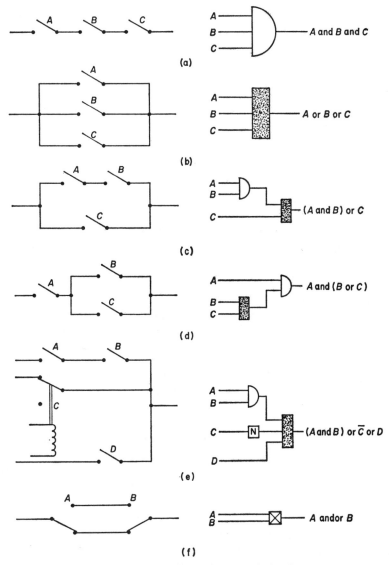

Figure 4.2   Examples of electrical circuits

whole circuit is ON when A and B are ON, or when D is ON, or when C is not ON. In (f) an ANDOR gate is shown; if the switches A and B are as shown (call this position ON), or if both are switched to the other position, the output is ON; but if one is switched OFF, the output is OFF.

CONTROL BY MEMBERS OF A SET

The notation of Figure 4.1 does not provide a convenient way of describing activities authorised by a majority vote, or by agreement between a given number of members of a group of controllers. Since these forms of control are common in administrative systems, a suitable notation for this purpose would be an advantage. For example, if two signatures of any three executives A, B, C are needed to validate a cheque, the procedure may be described as

$$(A \text{ and } B) \quad \text{or} \quad (B \text{ and } C) \quad \text{or} \quad (C \text{ and } A)$$

but more conveniently as $Z(2)$, which means that authorisation may be given by two members of set Z, where $Z = \{A, B, C\}$ (i.e. the set of A, B and C). Thus the notation $Z(x)$ means that only x members of a set need to agree on a given action, and $Z(m)$ requires a majority of the members of the set to agree.

Control for administrative systems

The linkages forming AND, OR and ANDOR gates conform precisely to the three control procedures discussed in the previous chapter. These procedures are:

1. *Control in series.* All the controllers connected in series need to agree on a course of action for it to take place. If one controller objects, he overrules the others. This procedure is designated as the AND gate.
2. *Control in parallel.* When controllers are connected in parallel, they all have to agree before an activity can be stopped. This procedure is a mirror image of control in series, but here each controller can overrule the others if he objects to the activity being terminated, and this is in fact the OR gate.
3. *Conjoint control.* Each controller can decree that action be taken or that an activity be stopped. In other words, when a controller acts he activates all the other controllers to whom he is connected in parallel. If he switches OFF, it is as if all the others switch OFF at the same time, and if he switches ON, they all switch ON. Here the last controller has the last word and annuls all previous actions of the controllers. This procedure is the ANDOR gate.

OTHER POSSIBLE LINKAGES *

Table 4.2 lists only three control procedures resulting from various linkages between two controllers, but there are many other possible procedures as can be seen from the exhaustive list in Table 4.5. Each procedure is concerned with four outcomes for the system, the outcome in each case being either state 1 or state 0:

There is one procedure for which all the outcomes are state 1,
$\binom{4}{3}$, namely four procedures, with three outcomes as state 1 and one outcome as state 0,
$\binom{4}{2}$, namely six procedures, having two outcomes as state 1,
$\binom{4}{1}$, i.e. four, having one outcome as state 1,
and one procedure for which state 1 does not emerge.

The total number of possible procedures is 2^4 or 16.

TABLE 4.5   Sixteen procedures for a two-controller system

Controllers		System																	
A	B	1	2	3	4	5	6	7	8	9	10	11	12	13	14	15	16
I	I	I	I	I	I	O	I	I	I	O	O	O	I	O	O	O	O
I	O	I	I	I	O	I	I	O	O	I	I	O	O	I	O	O	O
O	I	I	I	O	I	I	O	I	O	I	O	I	O	O	I	O	O
O	O	I	O	I	I	I	O	O	I	O	I	I	O	O	O	I	O

↑ OR   ↑   ↑ A   ↑ B ↑   ↑ B ↑ A ↑   ↑ NOR
NAND ANDOR | AND
NANDOR

A close examination of these procedures reveals that some include various operations in Boolean algebra, such as *negation* (the NOT gate, as in alternatives 10, 11 and several others), *conjunction* (the AND gate in procedure 12), *disjunction* (the OR gate in procedure 2), *equivalence* (this is the ANDOR gate in procedure 8) and *exclusive disjunction* (which is the negation of ANDOR, namely NANDOR, as shown in procedure 9). Furthermore, all the other procedures may be described in terms of the basic AND, OR and NOT gates. Further observations are summarised below:

Procedure

1. The system has only one state and there is therefore no need for controllers.

* Pages 77–85 may be omitted at first reading.

2. This is the OR gate (namely, disjunction) so that the procedure in this column may be described as *A or B*.

3. If the labels for *B* were to be reversed, the result in this column would be identical to that in the previous column, namely the procedure may be described as A *or* $\bar{B}$.

4. $\bar{A}$ *or* B.

5. $\bar{A}$ *or* $\bar{B}$. This is also the NAND procedure, namely

$$\bar{A} \text{ or } \bar{B} = A \text{ nand } B.$$

6. Here the system adheres to the state dictated by A; controller B is redundant.

7. The system is controlled by B; here A is redundant.

8. This is the ANDOR gate; also, note that

$$A \text{ andor } B = (A \text{ and } B) \quad or \quad (\bar{A} \text{ and } \bar{B})$$
$$= (A \text{ and } B) \quad or \quad (A \text{ nor } B).$$

9. This is exclusive disjunction and may be described as

$$\text{NOT(ANDOR)} = \text{NANDOR}$$

also: A *nandor* $B = (A \text{ nand } B) \text{ and } (A \text{ or } B)$

10. This is the reverse of column 7, i.e. $\bar{B}$.

11. This is the reverse of column 6, i.e. $\bar{A}$.

12. Here we have conjunction, namely the AND gate.

13. A *and* $\bar{B}$; this column is also the reverse of column 4, i.e. the procedure may also be described as NOT ($\bar{A}$ or B).

14. $\bar{A}$ *and* B; alternatively, this procedure is NOT (A or $\bar{B}$).

15. $\bar{A}$ *and* $\bar{B}$ = A *nor* B.

16. As in procedure 1, the controllers are redundant here.

BOOLEAN OPERATIONS

Tables 4.2, 4.4 and 4.5 suggest that Boolean algebra may be helpful for formal descriptions of control procedures and relationships between controllers. Consider the following Boolean operators[1,2] involving A and

Operator	Symbol	Meaning
Conjunction	$A \cdot B$ or: AB	If A has the value 1 and B has the value 1 then AB has the value 1, otherwise AB is 0.
Disjunction (also called 'alternation')	$A \vee B$ or: $A + B$	If either A or B has the value 1 then $A + B$ has the value 1, otherwise $A + B$ is 0
Implication	$A \supset B$	If either A is 0 or B is 1 then $A \supset B$ is 1, otherwise $A \supset B$ is 0
Equivalence	$A \equiv B$ or: A/B	If A and B have the same value then A/B is 1, otherwise A/B is 0

The operators *conjunction* and *disjunction* are also referred to as *Boolean* (or *binary*) *multiplication* and *addition* respectively. The rules of these operators are:

Boolean multiplication (conjunction)	Boolean addition (disjunction)
$1 \cdot 1 = 1$	$1 + 1 = 1$
$1 \cdot 0 = 0$	$1 + 0 = 1$
$0 \cdot 1 = 0$	$0 + 1 = 1$
$0 \cdot 0 = 0$	$0 + 0 = 0$

We can now construct a truth table to find the value of several expressions consisting of A and B, as shown in Table 4.6. The results are obtained by simply performing the operations of Boolean addition, or multiplication of the respective states of A and B (or their complements $\bar{A}$ and $\bar{B}$) in each row, as required by the operator in each expression.

TABLE 4.6   Values of some Boolean expressions

A	B	$\bar{A}$	$\bar{B}$	$A + B$	$\overline{A + B}$	$\bar{A} + \bar{B}$	AB	$\overline{AB}$	$\bar{A}\bar{B}$
1	1	0	0	1	0	0	1	0	0
1	0	0	1	1	0	1	0	1	0
0	1	1	0	1	0	1	0	1	0
0	0	1	1	0	1	1	0	1	1
Procedure in Table 4.4	11	10	2 ↑ OR		15	5	12 ↑ AND	5	15

Comparing the results in Tables 4.5 and 4.6 we find that

$$AB = A \text{ and } B$$
$$A + B = A \text{ or } B$$

The AND gate is equivalent to conjunction (i.e. the Boolean multiplication of the individual states of the linked controllers) while the OR gate is equivalent to disjunction (namely, it involves the Boolean addition of the individual states). Thus, the Boolean expression AB should be read as 'A and B' and $A + B$ should be read as 'A or B' (rather than 'A plus B').

If we examine the definition of *equivalence* we find that it coincides with the ANDOR gate, and if this operator is denoted by a stroke $/$, then A/B is read as 'A andor B' or as 'A stroke B' (but not 'A divided by B'). From procedure 8 in Table 4.5 it is evident that

$$A/B = A \text{ andor } B$$
$$= (A \text{ and } B) \quad or \quad (\bar{A} \text{ and } \bar{B})$$
$$AB + A\bar{B}$$

and this is easily verified by performing the Boolean addition of the columns for AB and $\bar{A}\,\bar{B}$ in Table 4.6.

Use of Boolean algebra

Operations involving several controllers obey the usual algebraic conventions, so that

$$A + B = B + A$$
$$A B = B A$$
$$A + (B + C) = A + B + C$$
$$A(BC) = A\,B\,C$$

also $\qquad\qquad A(B + C) = AB + AC$

similarly $\qquad (A + B)(C + D) = AC + AD + BC + BD$

It should be noted that the expression $A\,\bar{A}$ is meaningless, since it is impossible to require A and NOT A at the same time. Similarly, the expression $A + \bar{A}$ is not meaningful, since it requires either A or NOT A for the output of the system to be ON.

Table 4.6 also reveals that

$$\overline{A + B} \neq \bar{A} + \bar{B}$$
$$\overline{AB} \neq \bar{A}\,\bar{B}$$

In other words the negation operator, such as in NOT $(A + B)$, cannot be regarded as pertaining to each of the elements in the expression.

Inversion of Boolean expressions are governed by De Morgan's Theorem, which states that

$$\overline{A + B + C + \cdots} = \bar{A}\,\bar{B}\,\bar{C}\cdots$$

or

$$\overline{ABC\cdots} = \bar{A} + \bar{B} + \bar{C} + \cdots$$

Hence, to find the inversion of an expression (i.e. to perform the negation operation), the following rules must be followed:

1. each element in the expression is replaced by its inverted value, i.e. A by $\bar{A}$ and *vice versa*
2. each OR is replaced by AND and *vice versa*

Thus, $$\overline{A + B} = \text{NOT } (A + B) = \bar{A}\,\bar{B}$$

similarly $$\overline{AB} = \text{NOT } (AB) = \bar{A} + \bar{B}$$

and the two results may be verified from Table 4.5.

We now examine the procedures sometimes referred to as *exclusive or* namely that one and only one input must be ON for the output to be ON. This may be expressed as $A\bar{B} + \bar{A}B$, i.e. as $(A$ and NOT $B)$ or $(B$ and NOT $A)$. When the expression NOT $(A\bar{B} + \bar{A}B)$ is analysed and the appropriate substitutions are made, then

$$\text{NOT } (A\bar{B} + \bar{A}B) = (\bar{A} + B)(A + \bar{B})$$
$$= A\bar{A} + \bar{A}\bar{B} + AB + B\bar{B}$$

The first and the last terms are redundant, so that the 'exclusive or' is equivalent to NOT $(AB + \bar{A}\bar{B})$, which is NANDOR. We also find by substitution that

$$AB + \bar{A}\bar{B} = \text{NOT } [(A + B)(\bar{A} + \bar{B})]$$

so that all the following expressions to define the ANDOR gate are valid:

$$A/B = AB + \bar{A}\bar{B}$$
$$= \text{NOT } (A\bar{B} + \bar{A}B)$$
$$= \text{NOT } (A + B)(\bar{A} + \bar{B})$$
$$= (\bar{A} + B)(A + \bar{B})$$

As examples (c) and (d) in Figure 4.2 show

$$(A \text{ and } B) \quad or \quad C \neq A \quad and \quad (B \text{ or } C)$$

or, in Boolean form,

$$AB + C \neq A(B + C)$$

The right-hand side, which describes example (d), may be expanded to $AB + AC$, compared with $AB + C$ on the left-hand side, thus making the reasons for the inequality quite obvious.

It is clear from all these examples that, as in common algebra, the Boolean multiplication operation takes precedence over addition, so that there is no need for brackets in the expressions $(AB) + C$ or in $C + (AB)$; both are equivalent to $AB + C$. The most common conventions for precedence of Boolean operations are as follows:

NOT is performed before AND
AND is performed before OR
OR is performed before ANDOR

unless other priorities are specified by enclosing terms in brackets. Thus, in $A + \bar{B}$ it is first required to perform NOT B, then the OR operation (i.e. the Boolean addition), whereas in $\overline{A + B}$, which is the same as NOT (A or B), the operation in the brackets must be performed first. This convention for precedence of operations means that the expression (A and B) or C, which describes the control procedure for example (c) in Figure 4.2, may be simplified to A and B or C, but the brackets in A and (B or C) in example (d) are necessary to indicate that the OR operation should be given precedence.

When a controller appears in an expression several times, it is necessary to ensure that he is not asked to perform incompatible roles. A critical examination of a control procedure sometimes reveals incompatibilities and redundancies and allows the procedure to be expressed in a simpler form.

Examples

Consider the following examples:

1. *AA*

   A is required to agree with himself, hence

$$AA = A$$

2. *A + A*

   Either A or A can control the system, hence

$$A + A = A$$

3. *AĀ*

   $A + A$

   As we have already seen, these are meaningless expressions.

4. $AB\bar{B}$

As $B\bar{B}$ is redundant, it can be deleted so that

$$AB\bar{B} = A$$

5. $AB + A$

In the first term A is required to act with B, but according to the second term A can act on his own, hence B is redundant

$$AB + A = A$$

6. $A(A + B)$

Open the brackets and simplify

$$\begin{aligned} A(A + B) &= AA + AB \\ &= A + AB \\ &= A \end{aligned}$$

7. Similarly, $\qquad \begin{aligned} AB(A + B) &= AAB + ABB \\ &= AB + AB \\ &= AB \end{aligned}$

8. $A/B + A$

Substitute for A/B and simplify.

$$\begin{aligned} A/B + A &= AB + \bar{A}\bar{B} + A \\ &= A + \bar{A}\bar{B} \\ &= \text{NOT}\,[\bar{A}(A + B)] \\ &= \text{NOT}\,(A\bar{A} + \bar{A}B) \\ &= \text{NOT}\,(\bar{A}B) \\ &= A + \bar{B} \end{aligned}$$

Notice that the second and the last line yield the expression

$$A + \bar{A}\bar{B} = A + \bar{B}$$

which can be easily verified from simple computations based on Table 4.5, but this does not mean that $\bar{A}\bar{B}$ and $\bar{B}$ are the same! The ordinary algebraic subtraction and division operations are not valid as Boolean operations.

9. $A/B + AB$

Again, substitute for A/B,

$$\begin{aligned} A/B + AB &= AB + \bar{A}\bar{B} + AB \\ &= A/B \end{aligned}$$

10. Similarly, $A/B(A + B) = (A + B)(\bar{A} + \bar{B})(A + B)$
$$= (A + B)(\bar{A} + \bar{B})$$
$$= A/B$$

11. $\bar{A}\bar{B}(A + B) = A\bar{A}\bar{B} + \bar{A}B\bar{B}$
$$= \bar{B} + \bar{A}$$
$$= \overline{AB}$$

12. $AB(A + B) + \bar{A}B(\bar{A} + B) = AB + \bar{A}B$
$$= B(A + \bar{A})$$
$$= B$$

The last three examples demonstrate how expressions for rather elaborate procedures can be greatly simplified. The analysis of example 12 reveals that in fact A has no effective role to play in controlling the system and may be entirely eliminated.

13. $A/(B + C)$
This expression is A *andor* $(B$ *or* $C)$. If $B + C$ is first considered as a single entity, then

$$A/(B + C) = A(B + C) + \bar{A}(\overline{B + C})$$
$$= AB + AC + \bar{A}\bar{B}\bar{C}$$

and this result means that

$$A/(B + C) \neq A/B + A/C$$

14. $A/(BC)$

Similarly, $\quad A/(BC) = ABC + \bar{A}\overline{BC}$
$$= ABC + \bar{A}(\bar{B} + \bar{C})$$
$$= ABC + \bar{A}\bar{B} + \bar{A}\bar{C}$$

Possible procedures for the two-controller two-state system

All the sixteen procedures for two controllers handling a two-state system are listed in Table 4.5. This list is derived by enumerating all the possible outcomes for the states of the system and relating them to the corresponding states of the two controllers. It is not difficult to see that this is in fact an exhaustive list and covers all the possible combinations of linkages between the controllers. One way to enumerate all these various combinations is as follows:

		Alternatives	Procedure in Table 5
(a)	Outcome for the system is independent of the states of the controllers	I	I
		O	16
(b)	Outcome for the system depends on the state of one of the controllers	A	5
		$\bar{A}$	11
		B	7
		$\bar{B}$	10
(c)	Outcome for the system depends on disjunction of the controllers	$A + B$	2
		$A + \bar{B}$	3
		$\bar{A} + B$	4
		$\bar{A} + \bar{B}$	5
(d)	Outcome for the system depends on conjunction of the controllers	AB	12
		$A\bar{B}$	13
		$\bar{A}B$	14
		$\bar{A}\bar{B}$	15
(e)	Outcome for the system depends on disjunction of the linkages in (d)	$AB + \bar{A}\bar{B}$	8
		$\bar{A}B + A\bar{B}$	9

All the other combinations in (e) are already covered in (b) and (d), as can be seen from the results in Table 4.7. Each cell in this table is derived by

TABLE 4.7   Results for disjunction of the linkages in (d)

	AB	$A\bar{B}$	$\bar{A}B$	$\bar{A}\bar{B}$
AB	AB			
$A\bar{B}$	A	$A\bar{B}$		
$\bar{A}B$	B	$\bar{A}B + A\bar{B}$	$\bar{A}B$	
$\bar{A}\bar{B}$	$AB + \bar{A}\bar{B}$	$\bar{B}$	$\bar{A}$	$\bar{A}\bar{B}$

performing the Boolean addition for the corresponding row and column linkages. For example, the result for the second row and the first column is $A\bar{B} + AB = A(\bar{B} + B) = A$. The ten results (the cells above

4+

the diagonal are a mirror image of the cells below) include the four listed in (b) and the four listed in (d), leaving only two outcomes for (e). It can be shown that the outcomes for the system that depend on disjunction of the linkages in (c) have already been listed, and similarly that the outcomes that depend on conjunction of the alternatives in (c) or in (d) have all been accounted for.

SEQUENTIAL LINKS

A notable feature of Boolean algebra is that all the elements in an expression are assumed to act simultaneously, so that there is no merit in the order in which they appear in a given gate, thus

$$A \text{ and } B = B \text{ and } A \qquad \text{i.e. } AB = BA$$
$$A \text{ or } B = B \text{ or } A \qquad \text{i.e. } A + B = B + A$$
$$A \text{ andor } B = B \text{ andor } A \qquad \text{i.e. } A/B = B/A$$

In circuit theory the operation sequence of controllers is generally not important, since the final states of the controllers determine the state of the system, and this is illustrated in the examples in Figure 4.2. Also, there is no question of hierarchy in a procedure such as A *and* B; both controllers are equal in status and in their ability to affect the state of the system. This is not to suggest that they necessarily use this ability equally well, or that they act with equal frequency. If A is quicker than B to discern changes in the environment and reacts accordingly, then the procedure A *and* B results in B behaving comparatively sluggishly and A doing most of the work of switching ON and OFF. Nevertheless, both have *equal opportunity* in this control procedure, and this is what is referred to in the previous chapter as first-order control.

When we examine administrative systems we find that time-independent gates are not adequate to cover the variety of procedures that can be designed and it is therefore necessary to add the time dimension, or the sequence in which controllers are required to perform their duties. It is suggested that the requirement for such a sequence can be denoted by an asterisk in the control expressions (namely *and**, *or**, *andor**). This notation has the following meaning:

A and* B: A acts before B; if A is ON the matter is referred to B and if he is ON the output is ON, otherwise it is OFF; if, however, A is OFF, there is no need to refer the matter to B, because his action will not affect the outcome.

A or* B: A acts before B; if A is ON the output is ON and there is no need to refer to B; if, however, A is OFF then the matter is referred to B, who by switching to ON will overrule A.

A andor* B: *A* acts first, but whatever he decides the matter is referred to *B*, who may acquiesce or reverse *A*'s decision; the state of *A* signifies the state that he wishes the output to be at (i.e. he is ON when he wishes the system to be ON and OFF for the system to be OFF); the state of *B* signifies his reaction to *A*'s decision: *B* is ON when he approves and OFF when he disapproves, and the resulting state of the system is then derived from Table 4.2, where the state ON is denoted by 1 and OFF by 0.

Sequential links can be described by Boolean expressions similar to those used for time-independent links, except that an asterisk is added to denote the sequence in which the controllers have to perform:

$$A * B = A \ and* \ B$$
$$A +* B = A \ or* \ B$$
$$A/*B = A \ andor* \ B$$

The examples in Table 4.8 perhaps illustrate the way in which such a language can be used to describe administrative procedures. In these examples Z_1 is the set of n_1 known members and Z_2 the set of n_2 known members; the two sets need not be mutually exclusive.

It should be noted that for a given control procedure the correspondence between the composite state of the controllers and the state of the system is not dependent on whether the gates in the procedure are time-independent or sequential. For any given set of states of the controller, the result for the system would be the same, as can be verified by comparing the summary in Table 4.9 for sequential gates with that in Table 4.3 for independent gates. In other words, the algebraic rules for computing the outcome of any procedure which involves sequential gates are precisely the same as when the notations for sequential performance of controllers are deleted. But the sequential procedure allows a controller to be ignored, when it is evident that he can have no effect on the outcome.

Consider, for example, the following three procedures

$$A \ and \ B \qquad (1)$$

$$A \ and* \ B \qquad (2)$$

$$B \ and* \ A \qquad (3)$$

where the probability of *A* being ON is $p_A = 0.8$ and the probability of *B* being ON is $p_B = 0.6$; let us assume that the states of the two controllers are independent of each other. The probability of the system being ON is 0.48 for each of the three procedures. However in (1) and (3) *B* is required to be ready to act all the time whereas in (2) he is required to act

TABLE 4.8 Examples of control procedures

Example	Activity	Authorisation	Notation	Boolean notation
I	Payment of accounts	Director A or B or anyone of the group Z_1	A or B or $Z_1(\text{I})$	$A + B + Z_1(\text{I})$
2	Appointment of executives	Three members of committee Z_2, then approval by director B	$Z_2(3)$ and* B	$Z_2(3)*B$
3	Requisition of mate-rials	Any member of Z_1 or two of Z_2 or B	$Z_1(\text{I})$ or $Z_2(2)$ or B	$Z_1(\text{I}) + Z_2(2) + B$
4	Dealing with a custo-mer's complaint	Any two members of Z_1; if the complaint is dismissed, it is then referred to B, who may decide otherwise	$Z_1(2)$ or* B	$Z_1(2) + * B$
5	Major capital expenditure	Majority agreement by Z_1 but either A or B may overrule this decision	$Z_1(m)$ andor* $(A$ or $B)$	$Z_1(m)/*(A + B)$

only 80% of the time (since for the rest A is OFF and then the system is OFF, whether B wishes it to be at OFF or not). As for A, in the first two procedures he acts all the time, but in the third only 60% of the time. In reality, of course, the states of the controllers may be highly correlated, so that the probability of the system being ON may be much higher than 0·48, but the essential argument remains valid, namely that the sequential linkages AND* and OR* dispense with the services of a controller when these services are not expected to be effective.

TABLE 4.9   Results for sequential links

Link	Controller		System
	A	B	
	I	I	I
A and* B	I	O	O
	O	—	O
	I	—	I
A or* B	O	I	I
	O	O	O
	I	I	I
	I	O	O
A andor* B	O	I	O
	O	O	I

The definitions of the sequential links AND*, OR*, ANDOR* and the summary in Table 4.9 contain an interesting pointer to the way in which the state of controller B is to be interpreted. *In AND* and in OR* the state of B signifies the state that he wishes the system to be in.* From Table 4.9 it is clear that whenever B points to I the system is at I and whenever

TABLE 4.10   The meaning of the controllers' states

Controller	AND*	OR*	ANDOR*
A	State of controller corresponds to		
B	state he wishes the system to be in		I—if he agrees with A O—if he disagrees with A

B points to 0 the system follows suit, although—as we have seen—there are circumstances in which *B* is not called upon to act at all. *In ANDOR*, however, the state of B signified his agreement* (denoted by 1) *or disagreement* (denoted by 0) *with A's decision.* These observations are summarised in Table 4.10.

It should be recalled that the ANDOR (and likewise the ANDOR*) link allows *either* controller to change the state of the system. If, irrespective of the initial state of the system, *B*'s will must prevail in a sequential link, then ANDOR* proceeds as follows:

1. Suppose that initially the states are

A	*B*	System
1	1	1

An event occurs that requires *A*'s decision, which can be signified by 1 or 0, depending which state he wishes the system to be in after the event. When *A* has made his decision *B* can either agree (denoted by state 1) or disagree (state 0), and the results for the system are shown below:

A's decision	*B*'s reaction	Comment	Result for the system
1	1	No change	1
1	0	*A* considers a change unnecessary but *B* overrules him	0
0	1	*A* wants a change, *B* agrees	0
0	0	*A* wants a change, *B* disagrees; result: no change	1

2. Suppose now that the initial conditions are

A	*B*	System
0	0	1

After an event occurs there are again the same four possibilities as enumerated above.

3. Suppose the initial conditions are

A	*B*	System
I	O	O

After an event the four possibilities are:

A's decision	*B*'s reaction	Comment	Result for the system
I	I	*A* believes the system should change to I (he held this view prior to the event) and *B* agrees	I
I	O	*A* wants a change, *B* disagrees; result: no change	O
O	I	*A* wants the system to remain in its present state and *B* agrees; result: no change	O
O	O	*A* wants no change, but *B* overrules him	I

4. Finally, if the initial conditions are

A	*B*	System
O	I	O

the four possibilities would be as above with the same results for the system.

Thus, irrespective of the initial state of the system, the correspondence between the controllers and the system complies with that stated in Tables 4.2 and 4.9. This conclusion can easily be verified for the AND* and OR* links.

HIERARCHICAL ASPECTS OF CONTROL

The introduction of sequential links provides an interesting new angle of looking at some facets of hierarchical control. The link AND* implies hierarchy in the sense that in *A and* B* the controller *A* is required to act in the first instance, but for his action to take effect he needs *B*'s approval; if, however, *A* does not wish to act, the matter is not even referred to *B*. In this case *B* can overrule *A* only *when the latter decides to act*, but not otherwise, as shown in Table 4.9.

The link OR* has a similar hierarchical connotation, except that in

A or* B the controller *B* does not need to confirm *A*'s decision to act: but if *A* decides not to act, then (and only then) *B* is approached, and he must decide whether to uphold or reverse *A*'s decision. The link ANDOR*, however, requires that every decision of *A* be referred to *B*.

In addition to the way in which sequential linkages affect the participation of the individual controller in the decision-making process, they may well affect the type of decisions made by front line controllers. For example, in the procedure *A or* B* controller *A* knows that his decisions are subject to a close scrutiny by *B* only when *A* is OFF, and if he wishes to avoid such scrutiny his judgement may well be impaired, resulting in his decisions being more biased towards the ON state than he would have been, had he acted as a single controller. Such situations are not uncommon in administrative systems when the frequency of disagreement between *A* and *B* (when *A* is OFF and *B* is ON) is interpreted as a measure of *A*'s incompetence, or when *A* begins to anticipate *B*'s decisions and ceases to switch OFF if he expects *B* to overrule him.

It appears, then, that there are two distinct aspects of hierarchy. The first relates to the *relative frequency* with which a controller is called upon to act: if two controllers *A* and *B* are assigned to a system, *B*'s position may be considered more privileged if he need not handle every problem that the system is presented with. Controller *A* is the one to act in the first instance and there are matters that he can handle satisfactorily without reference to *B*, whose involvement is therefore less frequent than *A*'s. This is compatible with the definition of second-order control in a previous chapter.

The other aspect of hierarchy is that of *authority*, or the ability of one controller to overrule decisions of others. Thus, *B* may be regarded as superior to *A* if *B* has the authority to reverse *A*'s decisions, but not *vice versa*.

Consider the various linkages that were discussed earlier:

1. *Time-independent linkages*
AND—Each controller has the power to stop an activity.
OR—Each controller has the power to start an activity.
ANDOR—Each controller can either start or stop an activity.

Also, each controller can act as frequently as any other. There is, therefore, no special privilege (either in terms of frequency of action or in terms of authority) which any one controller enjoys and which is denied to others. Similarly, the procedure $Z(x)$ for control gives equal opportunity for all members.

2. *Sequential linkages* (for two controllers)
AND*—In *A and* B* the latter acts less frequently than the former;

also B can overrule A, but only for certain decisions of A.

OR*—Here the position is similar to the AND* linkage, but the type of decisions that are referred to B are different.

ANDOR*—Both controllers are called upon to make decisions in every case, but while B can overrule A (in A *andor* B), A has no authority to overrule B. Thus, B enjoys a privileged position of authority, though not that of lower frequency of action.

Clearly, then, time-dependent linkages introduce hierarchical control. AND* and OR* remove B from the front line and give him some authority over A; ANDOR* gives B full authority, but to exercise it he must scan *all* the decisions of A. It would seem that remoteness from the scene of action and complete authority are not compatible; to achieve the former, some of the latter must be sacrificed.

Sequential gates are, incidentally, relevant in designing training programmes. When a trainee A is connected to a trainer through an AND* or OR* linkage, only some of A's actions are examined by B, either those that are more important to the working of the system, or those for which A's training is considered to be incomplete, whereas the ANDOR* linkage calls for all actions of the trainee to be checked by the trainer.

THE MULTI-ROLE CONTROLLER

A controller need not be confined to looking after the performance of a single system or a single task. He may be assigned to control several systems, and his role may change from system to system or from task to task, and so may his relationships to other controllers change, depending on the control procedures in force.

Take as an example two controllers A and B who jointly supervise three systems and suppose the controllers are linked as follows:

for system 1:	A *and* B
for system 2:	A *and** B
for system 3:	B *or** A

The role of A in relation to B is different for each of the systems. In this example even hierarchical relationships are not maintained. In system 1 no hierarchy is specified, in system 2, B has a hierarchical advantage, but in system 3, A enjoys an advantage.

In establishing what hierarchical relationships exist between two managers in an organisation, it is therefore necessary to list their control linkages with respect to the many tasks that they are associated with; the wider the variety of such linkages, the more difficult it is to describe the relationship

4*

between the managers in a simple and concise statement. Such a state of affairs also raises the problem of the 'carry-over effect'. Human controllers do not behave like automatons that are capable of switching from one mode of control to another without any after-effects. An ambivalent hierarchical relationship between two controllers that depends on how they are connected at any moment in time may well lead to an erosion of the intended procedures, whereas a more consistent hierarchical relationship reduces the frequency with which each controller needs to switch and to adapt to a new role and this therefore helps to maintain the designed procedures.

MULTI-CONTROL PROCEDURES FOR THE SAME SYSTEM

For any given set of circumstances only one control procedure should apply, otherwise ambiguities may arise regarding the relationships between controllers and their system. This does not mean that all such relationships need be determined by a single procedure. There could be certain circumstances that require one procedure to be used and others that call for another. As long as the two sets of circumstances are mutually exclusive, only one control will apply at any one time.

Consider the following example: Two controllers are assigned to a system, but the linkages between the controllers depend on the circumstances, three classes of which are identified:

(a) Quality characteristics that define the performance of the system need not be too stringent and the control procedure is then *A or B*.

(b) Quality characteristics are not too stringent, but because *B* has many other duties to attend to, the procedure becomes *A or* B*.

(c) Quality characteristics are stringent and it is therefore necessary to institute the procedure *A andor* B*.

In this example two controllers are linked in three different ways, depending on the circumstances. It is as if a control procedure of a higher level is superimposed on the system. The 'super-control procedure' consists of a 'super-controller X' whose task is to monitor certain parameters of the environment and of the system and with the aid of this information to identify the class of circumstances that prevail (see Figure 4.3). If the class of circumstances changes, the super-controller switches to another state, which corresponds to a new control procedure that the two controllers should adopt. Thus, as long as class (a) prevails, the controllers behave according to *A or B*; when the super-controller perceives that the circumstances have changed to (b), he switches the controllers to *A or* B*;

and so on. There is a one-to-one correspondence between the classes of circumstances and the control procedures of the system.

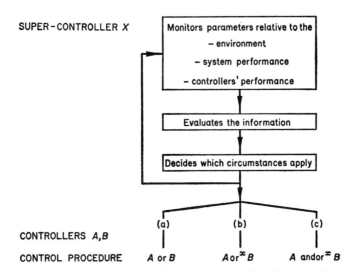

SUPER-CONTROLLER X

Monitors parameters relative to the
— environment
— system performance
— controllers' performance

Evaluates the information

Decides which circumstances apply

(a)   (b)   (c)

CONTROLLERS A,B

CONTROL PROCEDURE   A or B   A or^x B   A andor^x B

Figure 4.3   An example of a super-controller determining which control procedure to apply

MULTI-CONTROLLERS

As the number of controllers of a system increases, the number of possible procedures that can be devised increases very rapidly. In the case of a single controller in charge of a two-state system the number of states of the controller is two while the number of possible procedures is four, as shown in Table 4.1. For two controllers the number of possible combinations of the controllers' states is four while the number of possible procedures is 16, as listed in Table 4.5.

Consider now the case of three controllers A, B and C. There are eight possible combinations of their states, as shown below:

A	B	C
I	I	I
I	I	O
I	O	I
O	I	I
I	O	O
O	I	O
O	O	I
O	O	O

In general the number of these combinations for n controllers is 2^n and the number of procedures that can be enumerated for the system is $2^{(2^n)}$, and this number becomes formidable even for modest values of n as shown in the following examples:

No. of controllers	Combinations of controllers' states	Possible procedures
n	2^n	$2^{(2^n)}$
1	2	4
2	4	16
3	8	256
4	16	65536

The number of possible procedures is compounded even further when the concept of sequential links between the controllers is introduced, and naturally even further when a system with more than two states is examined.

In determining control procedures for administrative systems not all the possible combinations need, of course, be considered. For example, in the two-controller two-state system described in Table 4.5 two combinations (1 and 16) need no controllers and four combinations (6, 7, 10 and 11) need only one controller, so that the choice of a control procedure narrows down from 16 to 10 combinations and for possible administrative systems to six (AND, OR, ANDOR, NAND, NOR, NANDOR) or even to three (AND, OR, ANDOR). Nevertheless, the point should be made that for a system with a large number of states or controllers there is a plethora of combinations to choose from in the design of control procedures.

REFERENCES

1. Culbertson, J. T. (1958) *Mathematics and logic for digital devices*, Van Nostrand.
2. Hoernes, G. E. and Heilweil, M. F. (1964) *Introduction to Boolean algebra and logic design*, McGraw-Hill.

5 Notes on Information Processing

The first four chapters of this book are devoted to a discussion of the management task as a control process and to an examination of the relationships between controllers and the system they control as well as the relationships between the controllers. Most organisations are concerned with a wide variety of tasks, each requiring the participation of many controllers with various degrees of involvement. In order to handle these tasks and to maintain the necessary hierarchical relationships between controllers in the system, and indeed in order to pass directives and other signals between various parts of the system, a network of communications must evolve. When we observe an organisation in action, for example a manufacturing enterprise, we can regard it at a superficial level as a black box, the internal structure of which is disregarded, and make certain inferences about the enterprise by monitoring the physical inputs and outputs over a period of time. But if we want to learn something about the internal structure we need to examine the control function itself, and the only way in which the working relationships between controllers and those between them and other parts of the system can be passively observed (i.e. without asking the controllers to describe these relationships) is by scrutinising and evaluating the information flow in the system. No discussion of management control can be complete without some reference to information processing and this chapter and the next one are therefore devoted to this important topic.

THE MEANING OF INFORMATION

Information flow in a communication network is the lifeline of a business enterprise; it is like blood flowing through the veins and arteries of the body. It was Drucker[1] who said: 'The manager has a specific tool: information. He does not "handle" people; he motivates, guides, organises people to do their own work. His tool—his only tool—to do all this, is the spoken or written word or the language of numbers.' And because this tool is so essential to the working of the enterprise, large resources of personnel and finance are devoted to the development and upkeep of communication systems. That this activity is distinct from factory operations involving the production of a physical product is perhaps best symbolised by the term 'white-collar workers', with which we generally identify men associated with the production, manipulation and transmission of information.

No decision making, no purposeful control, no comprehension of what is happening in the world, is possible without information. If a decision maker has several alternatives to choose from, he can make a meaningful choice only if adequate information is available to enable him to evaluate the possible consequences of his decision. If no such information is available, he has no way of ranking the alternatives as to their possible outcome, and therefore has no way of making an intelligent choice, other than an arbitrary one. It is only by being able to *distinguish* between events that the decision maker can exercise control.

The following is probably a useful way in which information may be defined: *information is a statement that describes an event* (or an object, or a concept) *in a way that helps us distinguish it from others*. A garbled sequence of unintelligible signals is, therefore, not information since it cannot enhance our ability to distinguish between events, objects or concepts.

Different individuals may attach different values to the same piece of information. Information about changes in the stock market is important to financiers but of little value to production controllers in their official role (unless they happen to have a private interest in the stock market); an up-dated Atlantic weather report is important information for pilots flying over the Atlantic, but of little interest to pilots in the Pacific; inscriptions found in some archaeological excavations are generally far more valuable to archaeologists and historians than to botanists.

This is not, incidentally, the way in which information is generally defined by students of information theory, who are largely concerned with the *transmission* of information, in particular with the rate of transmission and with the quality of transmission. The rate of transmission has to do with the number of bits of information or signals that can be communicated per unit time and determines the capacity of the communication channel; the quality of transmission is associated with the errors that creep into the message, because of external or internal noise in the communication channel, or because of errors in coding a message at the transmitter's end or decoding it at the receiver's end (see Figure 5.1).

Classical information theory is, therefore, a theory of communications. It studies the effect of noise on the probability that the received message and the transmitted message are identical; it explores means for reducing interference between adjacent channels and other sources of internal noise, and means for increasing the rate of transmission through a given system. The theory is not concerned with what the message is about or how it is used in the decision process. In fact, information theory is not

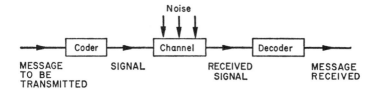

Figure 5.1   Transmission of information

concerned with managerial decisions at all; the only sense in which decisions are employed in the transmission activity is first in the design of the communication channels and input–output facilities, and secondly in deciphering received signals at the decoding stage to minimise the probability of error. But these decisions are quite distinct from the decisions made by an executive on receipt of the information at the end of the transmission process.

Production of Information

For management control purposes it is useful to distinguish between (see Figure 5.2):

1. data generating
2. data processing, and
3. information transmission

Data generating has to do with the measurement processes instituted by management for the collection of data that are likely to be used in controlling the operations of the enterprise. *Data processing* covers the activities associated with the data when they are available, including the organisation of data storage (so that the location of data can be easily identified for access and retrieval) and the required computational facilities (to provide means for analysing the data prior to transmission). The data are then transmitted to reference centres, where they are displayed or stored for future use, or to decision centres, where decisions about current or future activities of the enterprise are taken. *Data transmission* makes use of the communication network, which carries messages of all kinds; some are concerned with data in the strict sense of the term (which is associated with facts describing events, objects or concepts), others with decisions (directives to individuals or departments), views or proposals. A discussion of

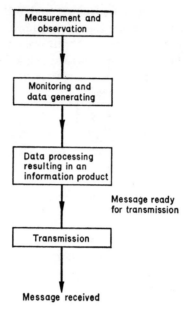

Figure 5.2 The production of
information

various types of messages in a communication system is given in the
following chapter, but it should perhaps be noted here that texts on
information theory are generally confined to certain technical aspects of
transmission and rarely view the wider issues of the communication system
as a whole.

Information as a Product

The terms 'data generating' and 'data processing' suggest that information is a product, similar in many ways to a physical product. First, there
must be a demand for it and some ultimate use to justify its manufacture.
Secondly, an information product needs to have specified its coverage, the
detail and accuracy that are required and the format in which the information should be compiled. The design and production functions
associated with a physical product are, therefore, useful analogies when
we come to examine in detail the activities that result in an information
product.

There are other interesting characteristics of information products,
which are reminiscent of problems in inventory control, such as:

1. *When to order*—inventory control of physical goods involves the
   need for replenishment, taking into account the amount of goods

available in stock, the rate of demand and the lead time that elapses from the moment the order is placed until the goods become available. In the case of an information product, the problems are similar; the timing is important in order to ensure that the information is available to satisfy future needs and account must be taken of the lead time required to produce it.

2. *How much to order*—as in physical inventory, too little information may not satisfy the need (and like the demand for a physical product, the demand for information may become stochastic), while too much information may be wasteful.

In production and inventory control of physical products, we distinguish between three types of goods:

1. *Perishable goods*—goods that lose all their value after a predetermined time period.
2. *Semi-perishable goods*—goods that lose some, but not all, their value with time.
3. *Non-perishable goods*—goods that retain all or the substantial part of their value indefinitely.

This categorisation is valid and pertinent for information products. News is usually a perishable good; it loses value rapidly as time passes and in that sense is akin to its physical relative, the newspaper. Last month's news flashes are of little value today, unless they are used as parts of a new product, such as a documentary, and this is like salvaging scrap physical products to make new ones.

Data about the performance of various parts of an industrial enterprise provide an example of semi-perishable goods. Sales statistics, quality control records, information on machine downtime, for example, become stale with time; for a while they still retain some value for the decision maker, but in addition to historical data he must have fresh information about recent events. Deterioration of this kind of information continues with time, until eventually the information loses all its value and has to be scrapped.

Some information may be non-perishable, such as records of historical events, archaeological finds, or literature and music of a certain quality. This kind of information never loses its value for historians, archaeologists, literature scholars and music lovers. In business operations, however, we are usually concerned with information which is perishable or semi-perishable in character.

Two main features that distinguish an information product from a physical product are first, that information is not 'conserved' (in the sense of conservation of matter) but can be available at different places at the same time; and secondly that the language used to describe a piece of information is the same as the language used to make the information product, whereas the language used to describe a physical product is distinct from the materials from which it is made.[2] Arguments that other distinctive features, such as that information is 'invisible', that information is for internal consumption, that information has its own identity, can all be shown to be invalid* or immaterial to the argument that an information product can be treated for management control purposes as a physical product. In the design of data processing and communication systems, this is the approach that systems analysts will usually take.

Control of Information

If we regard information as a product which has some ultimate use, then it follows that from the moment of its conception and throughout the stages of its production the needs of the user must be constantly kept in mind. The characteristic question that the systems analyst puts (or should put) to the manager is: 'What information do you need to control the business?' not 'What information do you have now?' A prerequisite to purposeful decision-making mechanisms in an enterprise is having the *right kind of information at the right place at the right time*, and this implies that clear specifications and objectives need to be prepared for each stage in the information manufacturing process.

This viewpoint also implies that the manufacture of information requires the institution of control procedures which are not dissimilar to those employed in the manufacture of a physical product. There is a need to ascertain that the information is indeed produced at the right place at the right time and that it conforms to specifications of quantity, quality and format. There is also a need to institute an evaluation procedure to review these specifications, so that information can be constantly improved and become better suited for its function as an important constituent part of the control process employed for the physical product and for the various activities of the enterprise. All this is reminiscent of the concept of control of control,[3] which has the task of monitoring, evaluating

---

* Information is 'visible' by the media on which it is transcribed; information is often produced for external consumption, and many physical products, such as components, are produced for internal needs; even in mass production physical products can retain their identity, and often do so by their serial numbers.

and redesigning control processes, and therefore includes the control of information.

The analogies that can be drawn between an information product and a physical product have prompted several writers to discuss the *economics of information*, the policies an enterprise should adopt in allocating resources to the production and disseminating of information within the organisation. Samuelson[4] suggests that economic problems are concerned with three issues: what (and how much) to produce, how to produce and for whom to produce. All these are certainly relevant questions to consider in the design and evaluation of information processing.

However economic analyses of production systems are mainly related to costs criteria, and this is one important aspect in which the control of information differs from the control of a physical product. Decisions on whether to make or buy components, on methods of manufacture (for example, costs can be reduced by employing inferior materials and quality standards), or on whether to retain the product at all, are often made primarily on a cost analysis. Such questions are largely irrelevant in the production of information, because information is not produced for its own sake; it is produced to enable management to control the enterprise. Because information has perishable or semi-perishable characteristics, the penalty for not furnishing information on time is not just the cost of producing that information, but the costs resulting in poor control of the company's operations, and these costs are difficult and often impossible to express in monetary terms.

It could, of course, be argued that once the specifications of the information product are laid down, they can be regarded as constraints, like specifications of any physical product that have to be met, and the systems analyst may then proceed to design the facilities of the communication system in the most economical way. In theory such arguments are valid; in practice they could lead to the design of rigid facilities guided by doubtful cost considerations, and there is a danger that the facilities would lack important features of flexibility and adaptability, which are so essential for an effective control process.

DATA GENERATING

The types of data generating activities can perhaps be best described by the matrix at the top of p. 104.

First, there is a distinction between *internal* and *external* sources of information. The internal sources emanate from the firm's own activities in such areas as sales, production and finance. The external sources relate to the general economic, social and business environment. In collecting

1. historical events
2. current events
   (a) time triggered
       (i) periodic time intervals
       (ii) predetermined, but not periodic
       (iii) random time intervals
   (b) event triggered
       (i) regular number of events
       (ii) prespecified events
       (iii) random events

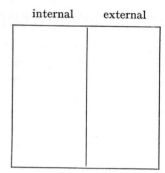

internal data it is common for the firm to rely on its own resources, to design its own means of collection and generally to have a wide freedom of choice in specifying where and how data should be generated. In the case of external data, reliance on the resources of external agencies is inevitable; there is a certain amount of data that the firm can collect with its own personnel or by employing consultants (for example, in conducting a market survey or customer reactions to products of competitors), but this amount is limited. The bulk of external information is derived from independent agencies, whose function is to monitor various parameters in the economy; here the freedom of choice that the firm has in specifying what data it needs is restricted to selecting from what is generally available.

The second distinction is between *historical* or past events and *current* events. Data on historical events are found in files and records, and provided they are comprehensive and detailed enough there is a good chance that management will find in them the required information. It is extremely difficult to forecast at the time of compilation of these files what may be required in the future. The experimenter or observer often finds himself in this predicament. He thinks he would need data to correlate variable y with variables x_1 and x_2 and he duly sets out to measure the three, only to be filled with regret at the analysis stage that he has not measured variable x_3, which he now suspects is the really important one. And to monitor everything within reach, so as to be on the safe side, is obviously costly and time consuming, as well as wasteful when it turns out that much of the data will never be used.

The monitoring of current events can be either time triggered, or event triggered, or both (as referred to in Chapter 1). Time triggered measurements and records are very common in industrial operations: reading instruments at given times (at regular or irregular, but predetermined, intervals), and periodic computation of data on staff, machines, sales, use of capital. Event triggered measurements are generated by prespecified events, such as: record details for every hundredth customer; read instrument A when B's reading is so much; count the number of pieces produced when the present batch of raw materials is used up; record when a given budget is used up.

Both methods aim at reducing the amount of data that would be generated if continuous monitoring is undertaken. Take, for example, a chemical process where temperature is an important variable. It can be continuously recorded on a time scale, so that subsequent reference to the record will reveal the temperature reading at any point in time. A time triggered recording will provide information for predetermined points on the time scale, with wide gaps in between (see Fig. 1.7).

An event triggered record will similarly have many gaps and will give only selected observations, but it will read quite differently from the time triggered record. The latter gives a better indication of the general average conditions of the process and it may well miss the crucial instances when action is required to adjust and control the process. The event triggered record provides data on extreme operating conditions and is therefore very useful for the purpose of taking swift corrective action, but the record lacks any detail on what is happening to the process under unusual operating conditions and therefore may have a limited value for subsequent evaluation of the control process itself. There are obvious advantages for combining the two procedures and having a record which is essentially time triggered, on which event triggered observations are superimposed.

Another method for reducing the amount of data generated by continuous monitoring is that of random recording; but it can be argued that random recording may be categorised as either time triggered or event triggered, depending on how it is specified. Taking a sample from a production line at random intervals is time triggered (by saying that a sample will be taken, for example, at times 8·01, 8·03, 8·10, 8·21, 8·22, etc.), whereas sampling from a population can be said to be event triggered, each unit of the population passing the recording mechanism being described as an event.

DATA PROCESSING

Many systems analysts differentiate between *information* and *data*. 'Information consists of data which have been measured, or appraised as good or bad and by how much, relative to a standard believed compatible with the objectives and goals of a business enterprise.'[5] Data are regarded as the raw materials from which information is produced, and in this sense the definition of information is again different from the one employed in information theory. The main purpose of distinguishing between information and data is to highlight the function of data processing.

Data processing consists of the following activities:

1. *data storage*
   (a) filing
   (b) retrieval
   (c) file maintenance
2. *data handling*
   (a) verifying and comparing
   (b) sorting
   (c) extracting
   (d) manipulating
3. *presentation of information for transmission as a message*

Data Storage

Records or items of data (and information) are stored in files. A file can take the form of a ledger, a folder, a set of folders, a card in a card index, a deck of cards, a paper or magnetic tape, a film, a set of ferrite cores in a computer core store, etc.

The term file, which is adopted from everyday office practice, already tells us a great deal about various storage activities and about the kind of specifications that can be made for storage media. When a piece of information arrives (i.e. a letter, a progress report) it must first be coded. In a manually operated office a search is then made for the appropriate file with corresponding code number, so that the information can be placed in that file. The recording in the file can be done in a chronological sequence, as is often the case with correspondence files, or it may be entered next to the data which it is mainly concerned with. If no file is found with the appropriate code number a new file is opened for this information, and for any future data bearing the same code.

Coding is obviously a key task. A wrong coding means that data are entered in the wrong files, resulting in a desperate and frustrating search when there is a need to retrieve the data or to refer to them, and this necessitates precise definitions for codes in order to minimise ambiguities and errors. Some ambiguities are inherent if the system of coding sets overlap. For example, it is common to find correspondence filing systems which have a set of files relating to institutions 1, 2, 3 etc., another set relating to individuals A, B, C, etc., and perhaps a third set relating to products I, II, III, etc. What happens when a letter is received from individual *B*, who works in institution 3, about product I? It could either be filed under B, or under 3, or under I, unless the coding specifies which set supersedes the others when overlaps occur, but this does not solve the problem that letters relating to the same subject matter, even to one particular transaction, are distributed among several files. It is, of course, possible to duplicate some material so that copies of the same document are deposited in several files. This method is effective in reducing the amount of search required for locating the material, but the gain is achieved at the expense of storage space. An intermediate method is to have cross-references between files, but not to reproduce the entire information in all the relevant files (this is often done in card indexes in libraries), thereby saving some storage space and restricting the search, but not eliminating it.

This procedure of distributing data to files is akin to the method commonly employed in storing physical products in a store. The store space is divided into compartments according to a predetermined classification scheme, and each product is accommodated in its appropriate compartment or shelf. Correspondence files in offices and libraries are generally organised in this way.

But it is possible to organise the store without this allocation of space to compartments. The product can be put anywhere in the store (for example, in the first empty space that is available), provided it can be found when required. In order to find it we need to scan the store until the name that identifies the product is encountered. This is, incidentally, what happens to a pile of letters before they are placed in files. To do away with the conventional correspondence files we could label each letter and to assist in our search we could have lists for reference purposes. Instead of having a file for all transactions relating to product I, we have a reference list, on which we note that document, say, 1234 belongs to the set in this list. Document 1234 may be mentioned in several reference lists. The concept of the list is not dissimilar from that of a file, except that it does not provide physical storage for documents; it merely specifies which documents (by code numbers, or labels) one should look for. Documents could be stored serially (e.g. 1234 comes after 1233), or chronologically, so that search and access become relatively simple.

Serial storage is common practice in computer facilities, such as on magnetic tapes which have the disadvantage of serial access, namely the reading head must scan everything that is stored on the tape before reaching the information it is looking for. With random access devices, however, the access time in modern computer facilities can be drastically reduced.

Another important task for data storage is that of file maintenance, which involves *updating* of data and *deletion* of obsolete records. These can be either event or time triggered activities (or both). The actual procedure employed for maintenance is closely tied up with the methods used to store data, with the total amount of storage available and the need to clear up space for future use, and with any restrictions that it is desirable to impose on the amount of information that should be made available for retrieval on request. All these considerations determine the amount of resources that must be made available for data storage management.

Data Handling

Four types of activities in data handling were mentioned earlier: verifying, sorting, extracting and manipulating. *Verifying* simply involves the checking of data that appear on different lists or emerge from different sources to see if there are any discrepancies or inconsistencies. Verifying is often carried out as a routine activity in conjunction with file maintenance, but there are also many verifying tasks of an *ad hoc* nature that data processing machinery is asked to perform.

Sorting involves the arranging of information in a prescribed order or format, for example: listing products in a descending order of sales income, listing employees in ascending order of periods of service in the firm, listing customers in alphabetical order. Naturally, the files which are being reshuffled by the sorting operation must contain information about the attribute that determines the final order in which the files are to be arranged.

Extracting, as the term implies, involves a search for selected information, or the scanning of a given set of data in order to identify a subset with predetermined attributes, for example: listing all the late jobs in a machine shop, listing employees who have served the firm for more than ten years, listing customers who order a particular combination of products. Extracting is the essence of management by exception; only those items which deserve attention or require action are singled out. If the information is recorded on cards, it is necessary to scan each card in the deck to ascertain whether it possesses the discriminating attribute, in which case the card is taken out of the deck (the original set) to a new deck (the subset), or the relevant information in the card is copied. The scanning may be a comparatively fast operation, if the information is properly coded by a series of holes and notches at the periphery of the card, so that the subset is extracted by means of a knitting needle inserted through the hole-location, or if a hollerith machine or a computer are used. Manual scanning and extracting, which do not take advantage of such aids, are usually tedious and liable to error.

When extracting involves several discriminating attributes, multiple scanning is generally required, and the sequencing of the scanning operations is somewhat reminiscent of the type of combinatorial problems that are encountered in job shop scheduling. Take the following example: from a batch of 10 000 invoices we wish to extract those that relate to a particular product (attribute A), that have been sold to a given type of customer (attribute B) and that have a given minimum monetary value (attribute C). The number of invoices involved in each category is summarised in the following matrix:

	A	B	C
A	1000	120	60
B	120	200	90
C	60	90	100

The figure in each cell gives the number of invoices that comply with the attributes relating to the corresponding row and column. The number of invoices after scanning for a single attribute is shown in the diagonal: 1000 if we scan for A, 200 for B and 100 for C. If we scan for A first, then the second scanning will reveal 120 invoices for B or 60 for C (see first column), and so on. The matrix is symmetrical so that scanning for A and then for B or *vice versa* yield the same result, namely 120 invoices that need to be scanned for attribute C.

The scanning of the original set of 10 000 invoices is inevitable, whatever procedure is adopted, but then there are six possible sequences that can be adopted:

A–B–C involving the scanning of 1000 + 120 = 1120 invoices
A–C–B 1000 + 60 = 1060
B–A–C 200 + 120 = 320
B–C–A 200 + 90 = 290
C–A–B 100 + 60 = 160
C–B–A 100 + 90 = 190

Where time spent on scanning is important, it is useful to adopt a sequence that involves as small a number of invoices as possible. In this particular example, the total number of invoices scanned (after the scanning of the original set) is derived by the sums of two figures in each row in the matrix, one figure being on the diagonal, so that the best sequences can be quickly identified. When the number of attributes is large, the problem becomes more involved, since the number of files scanned for each attribute depends on which attributes have already been scanned for. Another problem is that the number of files in a subset is often unknown before the scanning is undertaken, so that matrices of the type just described cannot be constructed unless some estimates can be made, perhaps based on previous experience. This is not the place to elaborate on this subject any further, but the example perhaps serves to illustrate the kinds of problems which are encountered in scanning and extracting operations.

Manipulation of data involves the use of available data for calculations and production of new information according to some predetermined procedures. Compilation of tables, handling statistics (of sales, production, employment, finance), or predicting trends (such as sales forecasting or growth patterns) all fall into this category. The purpose of such manipulations is to present adequate and pertinent information about past performance to assist management in the evaluation of this performance, and also to help explore future courses of action. This exploration can take the form of solving, for example, an allocation problem in production scheduling, or inventory problems in specifying reorder levels and reorder quantities; or it can generate a number of solutions with their computable consequences as a basis for further explorations; or it can stimulate a system and monitor its response to changes in certain controllable parameters.

These procedures for computation are the 'software' that we associate with a computer facility. They specify in detail the sequence in which the various computing operations are to be conducted. Such programmes are sometimes called by the appropriate name 'routines' (or 'packages') to indicate their anticipated frequency of use and to signify that once the logic and procedure of computation have been thought out, there is no need to reproduce them each time the computation is to be carried out; the routines will continue to be valid, until the need arises to modify or change them. Thus a routine is analogous to the setting of an automatic machine-tool designed to produce a given component; assuming that the setting remains unaffected by physical and environmental conditions and by the passage of time, the machine will repeatedly follow the same sequence of instructions to produce the specified component.

The product of data processing is now available, either for storage for future use or for transmission in the form of a message or a series of messages to various parts of the organisation.

Problems in file design

To summarise, the following are the main problems involved in file design.

1. The allocation of physical space to storage cells

With a given limited amount of space this allocation becomes an important parameter in determining the shape of an information system. Each storage cell has an address and can accommodate a file. As the cell-size increases, the number of permitted files decreases. Each file must then be designed to contain more material, and retrieval of information from that file takes longer. With small cells the probability that a cell becomes full is higher, so that files have to be split: at the end of a full file a reference and an address must be given for the continuation file (or files), and the continuation file must contain similar references.

The allocation of space to cells is reminiscent of the silo problem, where a given physical space has to be divided into compartments, each compartment being used for the storage of a commodity (such as some type of grain); when a compartment is full, another can be used for the storage of the same commodity, but no two commodities can share the same compartment.

An extreme solution to this problem is to have a single file, which is equivalent to having a single compartment, in which all the records are kept serially as they arrive. Unless there is a reference index that tells us where a particular record is kept (i.e. gives the address within the file), the whole file must be scanned before this record is located. For a large information store this method is obviously not very practical.

When the store has been divided into a number of cells, the address of each cell can coincide with the name of the file, if the file is to be permanently accommodated in that cell, so that when file 102 is needed we know that its address is in location 102. But if flexibility in allocation is desirable and if at some stage it may be thought convenient to move file 102 to a new location, then file name and location will not be identical and an index list is necessary to tell us where file 102 is located.

2. File organisation

The list of files, what topics they are devoted to, what information they contain and how they are linked—all these questions are closely related to the allocation of storage cells to files. Several types of files should be mentioned:

linear file—contains all the records pertaining to that file.

hierarchical file—different sections contain a different amount of details, designed to serve different levels of the management hierarchy.

inverted file—devoted to a particular topic which is included in the linear file, but not necessarily at the same level of detail (for example, the linear file may include information about all sales transactions, while the inverted file may deal with transactions of a particular product).

reference index—shows where individual records or information on certain topics are kept (in what file? in which location?).

chained file—to accommodate new material for which there is no space in the old file (for example, in a file listing customers in alphabetical order, if new customers have to be listed and if there is a shortage of space where the new records should be inserted, the addendum goes to a chained file with appropriate references).

File organisation determines the frequency of cross-referencing that is necessary and the amount of search required in retrieval of information. Inverted files, for example, are generally more economical for searching purposes, but as they duplicate some data that appear in other files, they add to space requirements and they involve more work in file maintenance.

3. Coding and reference

When a new record arrives, it must be properly coded and a decision must be made as to which file to send it to and where it should be placed in that file (if records in the file are not stored sequentially, the material may, of course, be duplicated and stored in several files). A sound method for cross references is an important factor in efficient information retrieval. Generally, the more cross references, the higher the probability of extracting all the required information, and the longer the time needed for search and retrieval. But it is not just the number of cross references that counts; the coding and reference schemes also affect access procedures to files and the sequence of search, and thereby its efficiency.

4. Maintenace

An information system needs constant maintenance, such as updating records and references, rearranging of material, restructuring files, as well as deletion of obsolete information.

5. Privacy and security

Privacy and security relate to two separate questions, the first to 'who is allowed to have access to a given file?' the second to 'who is allowed to change the contents of a given file?' These problems become increasingly important with multi-access devices and consoles located in executive offices with facilities for a conversational mode with a central computer facility.

Inquiries

One of the purposes of a data and information store is to be able to respond quickly to a demand for information. If the inquiry involves information that is already available in the required form and detail, then all that is necessary is to locate the appropriate files and sometimes (as in the case of a computer facility) to reproduce them. Often some processing is required, such as sorting and extracting, or even manipulating, before the inquiry can be satisfactorily answered.

There are many reasons for generating inquiries. Some are time triggered, others are event triggered (amongst the latter could be inquiries that are generated in response to reports transmitted by the data processing facility). Some are routine inquiries, requesting the same kind of information again and again; others are not.

Inquiries present a queueing problem for the data processing facility, and this problem is aggravated by the fact that event triggered inquiries arrive at random and that the time required to deal with them is variable. In order to provide good service to inquirers it is often possible, and sometimes necessary, to:

eliminate inquiries—time triggered inquiries can often be eliminated if routine reports, which cover the required information, can be generated in time; some report triggered inquiries can also be eliminated if it is found from experience what pattern the requested information usually takes.

anticipate inquiries—some time triggered inquiries can be anticipated if it is found that certain events generate certain requests for information; often some time elapses between the occurrence of an event and the triggering of the inquiry and this time lag can be employed to prepare information even before the arrival of the inquiry to the data centre.

reduce response time—inquiries often involve processing operations, such as extracting and calculating, using various given routines; some of this data handling can be anticipated by processing, so that information is produced and stored for the eventuality of its being requested, and much of this processing can be carried out in slack periods of the data centre; the reduction of response times alleviates some queueing problems at peak demand periods, but this is achieved at the expense of using more storage space, and with the risk that some processing will produce information for which no demand will materialise.

It is interesting to note that as we review the various activities of a data processing facility we cannot help noticing their similarity with many functions of inventory control and store management. In a warehouse supplying physical goods to a chain of stores there is a need to allocate space to items, to code items for identification and location, to have quick access and retrieval, to mix and prepack items in order to reduce the response time—all these operations have their analogies in data processing (although there are, of course, some important differences too) and these are useful in helping to define the problems that the management of a data processing facility is faced with.

INFORMATION TRANSMISSION

We mentioned earlier some technical aspects of transmission, which information theory is generally concerned with: coding and decoding, noise and error, channel capacity and other measures of performance. In addition, transmission is concerned with format and display: namely the manner in which information is displayed and conveyed to receivers. The written form (textual, tabular, or graphical presentation on paper) is the most popular medium at present in business, but there is an increasing use of the audio and visual media (tape recorders, telephones, films, television and other displays on screens). The choice of form depends partly on costs but mainly on response and transmission times, on the need for the receiver to react quickly and on the rate of obsolescence of the information (the higher it is, the more favourable audio and visual forms become).

All these are important issues, but the most important problem of all is who to transmit information to. We have already mentioned the fact that the same information has a different value for different people or departments, also that it has a different value for the receiver than that of the transmitter.

Obviously, it would not be feasible to transmit all the information that is available to everyone in the organisation, on the off-chance that every single bit is likely to be of some use; apart from the fact that the communication network will not be able to cope technically with such a load, no receiver could store, assimilate or comprehend so much information. The danger of the other extreme—that of transmitting too little information—is also obvious enough; nothing can be more frustrating for a manager than having to make decisions in the absence of vital information, knowing full well that the information is indeed available in the organisation, but has failed to reach him.

There is, of course, another important aspect to this: observations of the behaviour of managers leads one to conclude that some believe (rarely expressing their belief in explicit statements) that they retain power by withholding information from others. Withholding information restricts the possibility for delegation of authority, or for decentralised control. This is one reason for the resistance that is often encountered from managers to the installation of a computer to take over the processing of information relating to their work; they then may lose control over who the information is made available to, and this restricts their own room for manoeuvre and affects their role as decision makers.

The question of who to transmit information to is, therefore, not just an economic question. It lies at the heart of the managerial control process with inherent consequences to the organisation structure.

REFERENCES

1. Drucker, P. G. (1954) *The practice of management*, Harper and Row, p. 346.
2. Sisson, R. B. and Canning, R. G. (1967) *A manager's guide to computer processing*, Wiley.
3. Eilon, S. (1966) 'A classification of administrative control systems', *Journal of Management Studies*, **3**, 1.
4. Samuelson, P. A. (1964) *Economics—An introductory analysis*, McGraw-Hill, p. 17.
5. Keller, A. (1959) 'A flexibly automated, computerized information factory', Advanced Seminar for Professors of Business, IBM, San Jose, California.

6 Taxonomy of Communications

Communication is the vehicle of control. A communication system provides the means with which information, statements, views and instructions are transmitted through an organisation. Although we often speak of the 'flow' of communications, in fact this flow consists of a series of discrete messages of different length, form or content. These messages are transmitted through certain channels (or 'lines of communication'), which comprise the communication network; some of these channels are heavily congested, others are not. Each message is generated by a *transmitter* (an individual, a group, a department, a computer) to a *receiver* or several receivers. It may induce action or provoke a reaction in the form of a counter-message, or both. Every individual or department in an organisation acts as a transmitter and a receiver (though not for the same messages). Some individuals transmit more than they receive, others receive more than they transmit, depending on their role and function in the organisation. Messages in a communication network, then, are a manifestation of interactions in the system and of the control mechanisms at work.

It is not surprising, therefore, that many students of organisation theory have carried out observations of communication systems with the object of gaining a better insight into the organisation structures of the firms involved. A study of a communication network is, in fact, one of the few direct methods of observation that are available to a field research worker.* But it is perhaps relevant to point out that this direct observation is confined to messages transmitted in the system and not to the organisation structure itself. The structure cannot be directly observed. It is not a physical entity with tangible properties which the observer can

---

* Other methods involve observation of physical facilities, activities of personnel or the progress of a product through the firm; methods that rely on questionnaires or views of individuals can be argued to be indirect observations, in the sense that they reflect the perception of reality by those questioned and this perception is one stage further removed from the observer.

discérn or measure with the aid of any of his five senses. It is an abstract concept, which the observer can only hope to describe by inference, after examining the flow of messages in the network.

The organisation chart provides, of course, a model of the structure of an organisation, but almost invariably it is found to represent an idealised conception of what the organisation is like, or what it should be like, and this is why students of organisation theory have been searching for methods to record the informal structure, for example by drawing socio-grams to indicate the lines of communications in the system. Weinshall briefly reviews some of these methods and refers, for example, to the Formalogram (mutually perceived formal relationships chart, derived by matching responses to questions such as 'to whom do you report?' and 'who reports to you?') and the Informalogram (mutually perceived informal relationship charts, derived by matching responses to questions such as 'list the people with whom you work most closely regardless of their position in the organisation') and proceeds to describe the Com-municogram (which views the interactions between individuals and also the degree of agreement that exists regarding these interactions, both as to existence of the communication and to its character). Another example of recording verbal interaction between two individuals is given by Lawrence in his 'Interaction Scoring Sheet'.[2]

All these charts attempt to present a picture of the communication network in the system, each perhaps at a different level of perception, of the participants involved. The end result is a static picture, showing the lines of communications like a network of telephone lines, with perhaps some indication about the number of messages transmitted and received at the extremities of each line. There is generally no attempt to indicate the sequence or relationships between the messages or to record their character. Weinshall, for example, does include the 'type of interaction' in his study to verify the level of consensus among the participants as to what the messages were about, and to find out whether this consensus was higher for telephone messages than conferences. But apart from listing some types of interaction such as 'was the communication regarded as a decision, instruction, information, advice, or any other type of interac-tion?' he makes no attempt to define various types explicitly, while Lawrence[2] identifies four 'categories of speech': questions, information, opinions and suggestions or directions.

If control mechanisms in the system are to be identified, if it is thought desirable to trace the sequence in which a control procedure manifests itself through the communication network and is implemented, then a method of coding messages is clearly needed, and the purpose of this chapter is to provide such a method.

5+

CLASSIFICATION SCHEME

There are evidently many ways in which any classification scheme can be devised, depending first on the purpose which the classification is designed to serve and secondly on the level of detail which is thought to be desirable and practicable.

A fairly comprehensive classification of messages may be obtained through the use of four dimensions.

    1. Area of application of the message
    2. The nature of the message
    3. The importance of the message
    4. The intent and impact of the message

It could be argued that this four-dimensional scheme for classifying messages is not exhaustive, that there are still other facets and characteristics that remain uncharted. In fact it can be argued that no classification scheme of any kind is likely to be fully exhaustive, because by its very nature a classification relies on the definition of a finite set of entities, which must by necessity be limited, if it is to be at all practical, and that short of collecting all the messages intact, one is not likely to succeed in describing it fully (even then one would still need some evaluation, such as relation to intent and impact).

(A) AREA OF APPLICATION

This dimension is similar to dimension A in Table 1.1, where the areas of application are listed.

    1. Products or services ('the aims')
    2. Resources ('the means')
    3. Organisation structure and procedures

To these one might add two areas, which do not belong to Table 1.1 but which may well be the subject matter of messages flowing in the system.

    4. Evaluation of performance
    5. The external environment

It may be useful for some purposes to have a more elaborate list of categories. For example, the first two categories may be expanded.

    1. Products or services ('the aims')
      (a) Specifications and drawings
      (b) Quality and performance
      (c) Research and development
      (d) Prototypes

2. Resources ('the means')
   (a) Finance
   (b) Machinery and physical facilities; technology, methods of manu-
       facture
   (c) Labour and personnel
   (d) Materials and semi-finished goods
   (e) Production schedules and finished goods inventory
   (f) Marketing and sales

This list is given as an example of the kind of categories that may be considered in the case of a manufacturing firm. It is not meant to be a fully
comprehensive list; in certain industries, and indeed for non-manufacturing
enterprises, a modified or a different set of categories may be more
appropriate.

It is possible to consider this dimension with a further elaboration of the
time element involved. For example, in some cases it is convenient to
distinguish between (1) short-term and (2) long-term planning. This is
not the place to argue whether such distinctions are meaningful in particular industries nor to industry as a whole, and if so what time periods should
be specified in each case. This is merely to suggest that if and where such
distinctions are found to be useful, they can be easily incorporated into
this classification dimension, so that a message identified as 2(a2), for
example, relates to long term financial problems in the firm, whereas 2(c1)
is a message concerned with short term utilisation of manpower.

(B) KIND OF MESSAGES

This dimension is restricted to categorising messages into certain types
according to their form and to some extent according to the way in which
they are triggered. The main identifying characteristics are related to
whether messages are routine (that is, part of a well-defined procedure),
or whether they are *ad hoc*, also whether they are time triggered or event
triggered.

A *message* is a convenient general term to include all types of communications and may simply be defined as an oral or written communication sent by a transmitter to one or several receivers. The transmission of
messages can be done by one of three media:

written communication
oral communication in face-to-face meeting of two or more individuals
oral communication in telephone conversations

and some research workers have sought to establish the relative effectiveness of these media for a variety of circumstances.

Messages can, of course, vary greatly in character and form. There are reports, statements, inquiries, questions, accounts, comments, notes, records, retorts, recommendations, rejoinders, instructions, replications and indeed so many others, forming a morass of communiques flowing in all directions. Each may have a different purpose and a different role to play in the control procedures and may lead to different responses.

Written Messages

It is proposed that written messages may be grouped into six categories (see Table 6.1): routine reports, memoranda, inquiries, queries, proposals and decisions.

1. Routine report

A routine report is a message that provides information as a part of a laid-down procedure. There are two ways in which a routine report (or 'report' for short) can be generated:

    (a) time triggered, i.e. a report is called for at predetermined time intervals (example: a production manager is required to send weekly reports on faulty products or on idle time of machines)

    (b) event triggered, i.e. a report is called for when certain tasks are completed (example: a report is to be sent when a project is finished, or when consignments of goods are ready for dispatch).

In each of these examples the initiative to generate a report does not lie with the manager; the circumstances under which a report is issued are clearly defined in the procedures and all the manager is required to do is to ascertain that the circumstances that he finds himself in conform to these definitions. Even the contents of the report may to a certain extent be prescribed, either in the format that the report takes (as in the case of a designed form), or in the topics that it is expected to cover, although the manager can often exercise at least some initiative with regard to content and coverage.

2. Memorandum

A memorandum is a message that provides information, not as a part of a routine procedure. A memorandum can be in the form of

    (a) a statement of fact, submitted in response to an inquiry to assist in evaluating the situation, in preparing proposals for action or in decision making;

    (b) a statement which is event triggered, i.e. circumstances have changed in an unprescribed manner, calling for some initiative on the part of those concerned to draw attention of others to the new situation, so that an appropriate action, if necessary, can be planned;

(c) a comment, made in response to another statement or proposal, with the view of adding information or providing a new or different interpretation of data, generally with the object of amending a given proposal or making a fresh one; a comment can also be made in response to a request for information, when further clarification of the request is sought prior to the submission of a statement.

This is not to suggest that all routine reports are devoid of initiative whereas all memoranda are not. If a statement is made in response to a request, then the initiative for generating the statement lies with the individual who transmitted the inquiry, not with the one who responded. And although event triggered routine reports do not call for any initiative to generate them, there can be initiative exercised in composing them, whereas event triggered statements may not call for a great deal of initiative with respect to their content. Sometimes there is not even a great deal of initiative or imagination required to identify the event that should generate a statement. For example, in the case of machine breakdown or arrival of faulty material, such events could even be vaguely or precisely described as 'Report if you see anything out of the ordinary', or 'Report if the temperature reaches 500°C'.

But there is a difference between the prescribed event which triggers a routine report and the one that generates a statement: the first is described by *'when* an event such and such occurs, then, . . .' the second by *'if* the following event occurs, then, . . .'. The first describes events that are *expected* to occur; the second events that *may* occur. This is essentially the distinction between the circumstances that lead to reports and those that lead to memoranda.

The generation of a message containing information (report or memorandum) may involve one or several of the following activities:

(a) extracting data from available files, which are continuously updated
(b) processing data, including computations and analysis, on a routine basis
(c) collecting data on an *ad hoc* basis
(d) processing data on an *ad hoc* basis.

In the case of routine reports, activities are generally confined to (a) and (b), whereas memoranda may involve any of the four. The distinction between routine activities and *ad hoc* activities in transmitting information is useful in designing data-processing procedures and in determining to what extent they can be or should be mechanised. The distinction between (a) and (c) is helpful in evaluating information storage media and in deciding what data should be kept in a fast store with easy access, what may be kept in a store requiring only slow access, and what data need not be kept at all.

3. Inquiry

An inquiry is a note asking for information, to assist in evaluating a given situation, usually prior to making proposals for decisions. The response to such a request would be a memorandum, which includes a statement with the necessary information (extracted from available files or collected on an *ad hoc* basis) and perhaps an analysis of the data. The time lag between an inquiry and a response very much depends on the kind of data and analyses requested. If the data are available in a fast store and the available data-processing routines can cope with the required analysis, then the expected time lag may be comparatively short, while *ad hoc* data collection and processing can easily become the cause of serious delays. An inquiry would usually involve information not included in routine reports, unless these reports are time triggered and the information is required before the next report is due.

As mentioned earlier, an inquiry may meet with a comment, which asks for clarification or points out the difficulties in providing certain information in the time specified. Such a comment may be generated if the inquiry is badly phrased or ambiguous. But a comment is sometimes made by the person to whom the inquiry is directed when he wishes to play for time or to avoid the inquiry altogether, if he can help it. In response to such a comment, the inquiry may be renewed, perhaps in a modified form, or it may be withdrawn. The absence of a response to such a comment is often interpreted as a withdrawal.

4. Query

A query is a message stating the nature of a problem and asking for instructions or for proposals about courses of action. A query is often made by a subordinate drawing attention to situations which are not adequately covered by standing procedures, either because of the novelty of these situations, or because of ambiguities or inconsistencies in procedures. Sometimes the situations are not really novel, or the alleged inconsistencies in procedures are imaginary, but the subordinate may wish to ensure that standing orders are reinforced and reiterated.

A query may also be generated by a superior seeking advice and direction from his colleagues or subordinates. He may ask for proposals, which he can then evaluate before submitting his own, or before making a decision.

It is probably possible to make a distinction between a query relating to a situation that is covered by standing procedures and one that is not. The first is generated either because the questioner seeks reinforcement, as mentioned earlier, or because he is unaware of the procedures; the second involves genuine novel situations. But the line of demarcation may be difficult to draw in practice, and perhaps we need more evidence of its usefulness before attempting to suggest further definitions in this area.

5. Proposal

A proposal describes a decision that the writer suggests should be taken. A proposal can be drafted as a result of several exchanges of queries, inquiries, reports and memoranda; it may be drafted by a subordinate, at his own initiative or at the instigation of a superior or a colleague, or it may be generated by a superior wishing to test the reactions of his colleagues or subordinates. A response to a proposal may take the form of a comment (pointing out deficiencies, providing fresh evidence, voicing reservations or pledging support) and/or a counter-proposal. The absence of a reaction to a proposal is generally interpreted as tacit approval.

6. Decision

A classification of decisions is given in Table 1.1, where three dimensions are suggested:

dimension A: area of application
dimension B: routine scale
dimension C: relation to current state of the system

As shown earlier, dimension A in Table 1.1 is, in fact, a short version of the dimension 'area of application of the message', so that if the classification scheme outlined in this chapter is employed, only B and C need be considered here. The list of categories, of decisions given in Table 6.1 refers to the 'routine scale' (dimension B), but further categories pertaining to dimension C may be added if they are thought to be useful in monitoring messages that involve decisions.

A message involving a decision can take a number of forms: it may start with a preamble to review the circumstances that necessitated taking a decision to resolve certain problems; it may proceed by outlining alternative courses of action and explaining the reasons for the rejection of some; it may specify tersely what has been decided and how the decision is to be implemented; it may specify what reporting back is expected to keep the decision maker informed of progress in implementation; it may, of course, have any combinations of these ingredients.

Oral Messages

The same type of messages can be identified in telephone discussions and at meetings, but because of the rapid exchanges that occur when these media are employed, a special reference to them in the coding method is perhaps worthwhile.

Meetings

A meeting involves a discussion among several people, who participate either in their own capacity or as representatives of departments or other bodies. Meetings have four purposes: first, to reduce the time involved in other means of communications, so that exchanges can take place quickly; secondly, to provide an environment in which new ideas are stimulated by the rapid exchange of views and by confrontation of individuals (two elements that are often missing in a communication system that relies on written messages); thirdly, to reduce the amount of storage of information (the deliberations of a meeting can be summarised and stored more economically than the equivalent amount of written statements); and fourthly, to get the individuals attending the meeting more committed to given proposals or procedures than they would perhaps otherwise be. These purposes are not listed in their order of merit; their relative importance will obviously depend on circumstances.

There are two kinds of meetings.

1. *Routine*, such as meetings of standing committees
2. *Ad hoc*, called to discuss particular issues.

The distinction between *routine* and *ad hoc* meetings is like the distinction between a routine report and a memorandum. Like a routine report, a routine meeting can be either time triggered or event triggered, while an *ad hoc* meeting may be called in response to a request to look at a particular problem with given terms of reference, or it may be event triggered, or it may be called to examine a given report or statement with the view of commenting on it.

A meeting may result in issuing any one or several of the messages listed earlier: it may issue a routine report (if it is routine meeting) or a memorandum; it may generate an inquiry for further information; it may ask for instructions; it may produce proposals, or it may generate decisions. But a meeting can also fizzle out, if after many deliberations it ends inconclusively.

In any particular meeting the exchanges themselves can be examined and coded in terms of the six categories listed earlier. For example, a meeting may start with a routine report, followed by a succession of verbal inquiries and verbal statements, and conclude with a set of proposals. An observer present at such a meeting may wish to record in detail these exchanges and code them accordingly, so that the flow of information and the nature of the exchanges can be subsequently analysed in greater detail. In fact, every utterance, every sentence, even every part of a written or verbal message, can be analysed in the same way. But for many applications such a detailed record may not be needed and it may be sufficient to note that a meeting has taken place.

The level of detail with which events in the communication system are recorded is a matter of choice for the investigator or analyst, like the scale chosen for a map or a photograph : the larger the scale, the greater the detail, the more extensive the records needed to cover a given area and the greater the amount of effort needed to compile the records. In short, the investigator must decide on how far he is prepared to lose sight of the wood for the sake of getting a better view of the trees. But the important point to make is that the categorisation of messages proposed here can be used both for macro- and micro-analyses, thereby providing complete freedom in conducting studies of communication systems in different depth and with a flexible frame of reference.

At a macro-analysis level, where a whole message is considered, it is sometimes difficult to characterise it with a single coding. The message may consist of several ingredients (for example, it may cover a report, a query and a proposal) and have to be coded accordingly. It must be recognised that the investigator will have to exercise his judgement under these circumstances, and he may well have to examine the purpose of the message in order to assign the most relevant coding to it.

Telephone discussion

Many of the comments made on meetings are relevant to telephone communications. The distinction made earlier between routine and *ad hoc* communications may be useful here and the discussion about the level at which an analysis is aimed is just as pertinent. As in the case of a meeting, it may suffice to record the fact that a telephone conversation has taken place and code it according to the most significant outcome, or it may be necessary to examine the exchanges in greater detail. There are some obvious differences between the two media : a telephone conversation is generally restricted to two participants, it lacks certain facets of interaction that can be found in a face-to-face exchange, and it poses some technical problems for the investigator who wishes to record and analyse the conversation in some detail.

COMMUNICATION CHART

The *comchart* (communication chart) is a useful tool for recording patterns of communications by coding messages and charting their flow and

5*

sequence. The comchart is task oriented and is somewhat reminiscent of the tracer method used by industrial engineers in work study or plant layout investigations. The suggested codes are shown in Table 6.1.

TABLE 6.1   Coding Scheme for Messages

Crude coding	More detailed
R—routine report	$R1$—time triggered report $R2$—event triggered report
M—memorandum	S—statement, following an inquiry, or event trig-gered C—comment Details on data collection and processing can be added as follows:* 1—data from available records 2—*ad hoc* data collection 3—routine data processing 4—*ad hoc* processing
I—inquiry	$I1$—inquiry covered by standing procedures $I2$—inquiry regarding a novel situation, not ade-quately covered by standing procedures
Q—query	$Q1$—query when the problem is covered by pro-cedures $Q2$—query for novel situations, or to clear ambigui-ties and inconsistencies
P—proposal	$P1$—proposal regarding procedures or recurrent events $P2$—proposal on an *ad hoc* issue
D—decision	Using dimension B in Table 1.1:† $D1$—routine decision (high replication, high fre-quency) $D2$—high replication, low frequency $D3$—low replication, high frequency $D4$—*ad hoc* decision (low replication, low fre-quency)

H—meeting, the outcome of which may be any one or several of the above codes; if the meeting fizzles out, the result is denoted by O.

T—telephone discussion

* The particular kind of memorandum may be coded in this way, such as $S1$, $C3$, etc.
† Similarly, dimension C in Table 1.1 may be added.

An example of a comchart is shown in Table 6.2 (and a case study cited elsewhere[3]). The executives and/or departments participating in the exchange of messages are listed at the top and the relevant committees are shown separately. Executive 1 generates a query to executive 2, who then

TABLE 6.2   A comchart

generates inquiries by telephone (T shown in parentheses) through executives 3, 4 and 5. Executive 4 sends a memorandum to 3, while 5 sends one coupled with an inquiry to 6, who responds with a memorandum. A meeting involving 3, 5 and 7 takes place, resulting in a memorandum sent by 3 (the convenor of the meeting) to 2, who after receiving a routine report from committee G1 and a memorandum and proposals from G2, meets 3 and receives a memorandum from him (committee G3 also discusses the issue, but has nothing to contribute). Executive 2 then sends in his own proposals to 1. Executive 1 then formulates his decision, but first he tests 2, 3 and 4 by sending them his draft proposals and in the absence of any comments, issues his instructions.

The sequence of events in the chart is perfectly clear : each row denotes an event—message or meeting—and all the events are listed in their chronological order, the connection between two consecutive events being shown by the vertical line drawn between them. This line can be used to indicate with whom the next move is expected to lie, and it can be seen from the chart that this vertical line is in most cases followed by the transmission of a fresh message or by convening a meeting. In two cases in the chart messages were expected from executive 7 and from committee G3 in rows 5 and 7 respectively, but both failed to generate anything.

The time scale can be indicated on the vertical axis, as shown in the chart (using appropriate time units, such as hours, days, weeks, etc.), so that the time elapsed between any two events can be easily computed (alternatively, the chart can be drawn to a linear time scale, if this is thought to be more convenient).

The chart also makes it clear who the transmitter and who the receiver are. In the first three rows this is shown by an arrow, but if we use the convention that the code for each message is recorded in the column of the transmitter, then the arrow can be dispensed with, as seen in subsequent rows. The nodes in each row indicate who is involved in any message or meeting, and in the case of the latter the symbol H is shown in the column of the convenor (for example, on day 15 executive 3 convened a meeting in which 5 and 7 took part; on day 29 executive 2 called 3 for a meeting). The convenor need not necessarily be the transmitter of the next message (as shown by these two examples in the chart).

The comchart, therefore, can be an effective tool for recording a sequence of events pertaining to any particular task and provide a useful basis for identifying control mechanisms in the system and for analysing interrelationships. It also provides a means of relating messages to a time scale, of locating delays, and of showing the role that individuals play in the communication network. But it is, of course, only an aid to analysis, not analysis itself. The investigator must still decide on the detail with which the comchart should be recorded, the point in time at which to start and the point at which to end, and above all the subject of the chart and the way in which the task is to be traced. All these decisions relate to the conduct of the study, largely even before the recording has begun. Like a film director, the investigator still needs to supervise the shooting itself, and of course to spend the many agonising hours in the cutting room.

ANALYSIS OF ROLES

The comchart gives some indication of the roles assumed by various individuals or departments in the progress of any particular task, but it may sometimes be useful to consider an array of tasks, such as the summary shown in Table 6.3. Each row is devoted to one task and attempts to

TABLE 6.3   Task tableau

Task	Executives						
	1	2	3	4	5	6	7
1	Q, D	I	P	M	M		
2	I		P	M	M	M	M
3		D	Q			M	
4		D	P			M	
5	D	Q	P		M		

summarise the information recorded in the comchart related to that task, so that the type of the *main messages transmitted* by each participant is shown. Thus, the summary shows the main roles that each participant assumes: some mainly generate memoranda, others make proposals, and so on.

TABLE 6.4   Role chart

Time	Executives						
	1	2	3	4	5	6	7
1	Q	(Q)					
		I, T	(I, T)	(I, T)	(I, T)		
2				(M)		M	
			(M)	(M)			M
3	H	(H)	(H)				
4		Q, I	(Q)		(I)	(I)	(I)
5	(P)	P					
					H	(H)	(H)
6	D	(D)	(D)				
7		D		(D)	(D)	(D)	

It is obviously not always easy to summarise a whole comchart, particularly when it is long and intricate, into a single row, and some alternative record, which is executive oriented rather than task oriented, may be considered more pertinent for analysis of roles, in which case a

role chart—such as the one shown in Table 6.4—may be useful. Interactions are recorded as they are experienced by the executives on a time
scale; if necessary each row devoted to one interaction. A symbol without
parentheses denotes a transmitter, one with parentheses stands for a
receiver (with the exception of the symbol T, which is given in parentheses
to indicate telephone messages; H denotes a convenor of a meeting and (H)
stands for a participant in a meeting). Glancing down a column we can
often form a quick impression of the role of the corresponding individual
in the time considered.

THE ROLE OF THE COMPUTER

The important position that a computer can assume in a communication network raises the question of its possible role in the organisation
structure. The computer is often regarded as a means of storing and processing data. Apart from input and output devices, it is made of two parts:
a store, which consists of files of information suitably organised for easy
access, and a processing unit, which carries out the computations or
manipulations described in the programmes fed into the computer. These
programmes may specify the format in which data retrieved from storage
are to be presented (for example, listing invoices or financial balances) or
they may prescribe how data should be scanned so that only certain bits
of information are extracted and highlighted for further attention (for
example, listing items with stocks below predetermined levels), or they
may include routines for using available information in order to generate
new data (for example, forecasting).

It is therefore natural to regard the computer as a receiver and a transmitter of reports and memoranda and, of course, as a receiver of inquiries—
a kind of miniature filing system with rapid access and fast input–output.
But the computer can be much more than that and there is no reason why
it should not transmit queries and inquiries, generate proposals or take
decisions. Such roles can be designed and incorporated in appropriate
software and an analysis of a communication system which includes a
computer can be aided by the use of comcharts and role charts.

(C) IMPORTANCE OF MESSAGES

The investigator of systems and procedures is often struck by the
multitude of messages that flow between different parts of an organisation.
Some are vital messages, either for the day-to-day control of operations or
for decisions that affect the future of the enterprise, others are less significant, even trifling. In order to understand or evaluate control mechanisms

in an organisation it is obviously useful to be able to distinguish between the important and the trivial, and it is conceivable that some hierarchy of importance can be devised as a basis for classifying messages.

It is difficult, if not impossible, to suggest a universal prescription on how to devise an 'importance scale' for messages. The degree of importance that one attaches to any event in life is a subjective matter. And who is to judge? Also, the same message viewed by the same person may assume a different level of importance at different times. Far too often a message is considered to be very important at the time of transmission, but may be regarded as trivial after the event.

Assuming that the purpose of sending a message is to have some impact on the receiver and that the purpose of coding it is to gain some insight into the control process in the organisation, it is reasonable to suggest that if a message is to be put on an 'importance scale' the transmitter and the receiver of the message should rank the message separately at the time of its transmission or receipt. The evaluation of the message by the transmitter is likely to be very different from that of the receiver and to rely solely on the coding of either is bound to produce a one-sided view of the role of the message in influencing subsequent events.

Another relevant element is the hierarchical relationship between the transmitter and the receiver. If the transmitter of a message belongs to a higher echelon in the organisation hierarchy than the receiver, then the latter is more likely to attribute a high level of importance to the message than the former. Similarly, in transmitting a message to a higher authority, the transmitter is likely to take the message very seriously and (except for cases of emergencies) this fact manifests itself in the comparatively long time that the transmitter takes to compose the message.

In any given function of management, or in any given area of application, routine messages are likely to be regarded as less important than *ad hoc* messages. As *ad hoc* messages are essentially all event triggered, they generally receive more attention than time triggered messages, although there may be here some notable exceptions, such as periodic accounts which are usually regarded by managers as important documents.

The expected reaction time is another ingredient that may be used in an 'importance scale'. The quicker the transmitter expects the receiver to react to the message, the greater the importance the transmitter is likely to attach to it. And the quicker the receiver does react or wishes to react, the more important the message is likely to be regarded by him.

These are just a few factors that may be considered as useful in the construction of a measure of importance for messages, starting with a crude mapping scheme such as the one given in Table 6.5.

Some zealous investigators may wish to follow this up by many refinements, and even to explore ways of reducing the various factors to a single measure by an appropriate weighting procedure; others may be content to leave the transmitter and the receiver to rank messages on a global scale without a detailed breakdown into various attributes. What is perhaps relevant is that a measure of importance for messages cannot be set up

TABLE 6.5   Importance of messages

Importance level	high	low
Message from/to an individual with a	higher status	lower status
Generation of the message	event triggered	time triggered
Expected reaction time	fast	slow

independently of the other three dimensions of the classification scheme. Clearly, the importance of a message may well depend on dimension (a), namely on the area of application. The kind of message, as described by dimension (b), as well as the intent and impact of the message in dimension (d), are very pertinent to the importance of the message. Indeed, it may even be argued that a measure of importance may be inferred from the other dimensions and that there is no need to consider it separately.

(D) INTENT AND IMPACT

Apart from its technical and informative content, a message may be transmitted with some intention in mind, such as to cause an action to be taken, to convey encouragement, criticism, rebuke, provocation. The impact on the receiver may be entirely different from the one intended, and this is why a description of the message in terms of intent and impact may provide an additional insight into behaviour in organisations.

One way to describe intent is to differentiate between messages that are related to actions and those that are related to attitudes of the receiver. Another categorisation is the distinction between messages that are intended to maintain the *status quo* and those that seek to change it.

This suggested classification matrix is described in Table 6.6. A message categorised as $A1$ seeks to maintain an existing activity, namely it reiterates the transmitter's view that the activity should continue at its present level and in its present form, whereas $A2$ seeks to change it. This classification is reminiscent of the one suggested for decisions in Table 1.1, where a further elaboration is given on the type of change that the decision attempts to achieve: a change effected by modifying an existing activity, or by stopping it altogether, or by starting a new one.

With respect to attitudes it may be desirable to distinguish between three types: the attitude of the receiver to the transmitter, his attitude towards other people, or his attitude to the organisation.

Table 6.6 applies equally to the description of a message in terms of intent or in terms of impact. Thus, if a message is classified as $A2(1)$ for

TABLE 6.6   Intent/impact

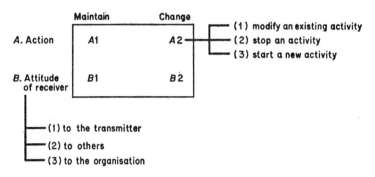

intent but as $A1$ for impact, then clearly the transmitter has not been successful in conveying his purpose to the receiver.

As in the classification scheme for other dimensions, it is possible here for a message to fall into more than one category, but if it transpires that too many messages belong to too many categories, then the classification ceases to be sufficiently discriminating and may have to be abandoned.

CONCLUSION

There is no attempt in this proposed taxonomy of communications to describe messages as to their thoroughness, excellence, ingenuity, or to provide an objective assessment of their psychological impact or importance. Some reports or memoranda may be keystones in deliberations leading to decisions, others may be trivial by comparison; some proposals may exhibit brilliance and far-sightedness, others may be pretty mundane and represent just 'noise' in the communication system. The comchart as shown in Table 6.2, and the other dimensions of the classification discussed do not show any of this. They merely identify and record messages in their sequential setting according to certain attributes.

But an interpretation and evaluation of the chronicle still requires a historian. It may be argued, of course, that the historian's task could be made easier by the chronicler providing information beyond the mere recording of events, but there is no systematic procedure for assessing events as they occur that we can yet suggest for the chronicler to use. This is not to say that the proposed taxonomy and charts cannot be improved, and as we gain more experience in recording and in evaluation (most investigators in this field combine the roles of chroniclers and historians) no doubt our methods will become more refined, more intricate, and—let us hope—more useful for the analysis of organisations.

REFERENCES

1. Weinshall, T. D. (1966) 'The communicogram', *Operational research and the social sciences*, edited by J. R. Lawrence, Tavistock Publications, London, pp. 619–633.
2. Lawrence, P. R. (1958) *The changing pattern of organizational behavior patterns—a case study of decentralization*, p. 231, Harvard.
3. Eilon, S. (1968) 'Taxonomy of communications', *Administrative science quarterly*, 13, 2, pp. 281–4.

7 What is a Decision?

Let us now return to the theme of viewing the management task as a control process. We have seen how the manager can be regarded as a controller employing a closed loop process, how he can monitor the behaviour of the system and how he communicates with parts of the system and with his fellow controllers. In Chapter 1 the controller is identified as a decision maker, since it is through his decisions transmitted to the system that he can adjust its performance and steer it along a desirable course. A decision is the culmination of the control process, the final stage in the analysis of information and the evaluation of possible courses of action. In Chapter 1 a brief classification of various types of decisions is suggested, but let us now turn our attention to the decision process itself. What is a decision? To what extent is it and can it be routinised and mechanised? These are the questions which occupy us in this chapter and in the next one.

DEFINITIONS

An examination of the literature reveals the somewhat perplexing fact that most books on management and decision theory do not contain a specific definition of what is meant by a *decision*. One can find detailed descriptions of decision trees, discussions of game theory and analyses of various statistical treatments of payoff matrices under conditions of uncertainty, but the definition of the decision activity itself is often taken for granted and is associated with making a choice between alternative courses of action. As Fishburn puts it:

> Solving the decision model consists of finding a strategy for action, the expected relative value of which is at least as great as the expected relative value of any other strategy in a specified set. The prescriptive criterion of a strategy will be maximisation of the decision maker's total expected relative value.[1]

A concise description of alternative definitions of a decision is given by Ofstad, who says:

> To say that a person has made a decision may mean (1) that he has

started a series of behavioral reactions in favor of something, or it may mean (2) that he has made up his mind to *do* a certain action, which he has no doubt that he ought to do. But perhaps the most common use of the term is this: 'to make a decision' means (3) to make a judgment regarding what one *ought* to do in a certain situation after having deliberated on some alternative courses of action.[2]

He then adds that (3) has the support of philosophical tradition. To quote Churchman,

The manager is the man who decides among alternative choices. He must decide which choice he believes will lead to a certain desired objective or set of objectives.[3]

The essential ingredients in this definition are that the decision maker has several choices and that his choice involves a *comparison* between these choices and the *evaluation* of their outcomes.

THE DECISION PROCESS

Before we concentrate on the final selection of a course of action, it is necessary to consider the decision activity as a whole. What are the mental processes that the decision maker goes through before he arrives at his conclusion?

Figure 7.1 is an attempt to describe the decision process in a schematic form: First, there is an information input, say from some data-processing machinery. This is followed by an analysis of the information to ascertain its validity and discriminate between its significant and insignificant parts. The analysis leads to the specification of performance measures, which provide the basis for determining how a particular course of action is to be judged, and then to the construction of a model in order to describe the behaviour of the system for which the manager is asked to make a decision.

In a production-marketing system, for example, the measures of performance may include profit, mean level and/or variance of plant utilisation, level of meeting customer demand, and so on. Thus, any given courses of action, whether they represent existing policies or whether they are hypothetical propositions for new policies, can be described by arrays of the measures of performance that are thought to be most relevant.

A set of possibilities (or 'strategies' in the language of the theory of games) is enumerated and predictions are then made regarding the possible outcomes of each possibility. In order to be able to select between them, a criterion for comparing outcomes in the light of their respective measures of performance is set up and finally the selection (called here *resolution*) is made.

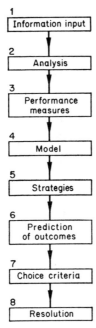

Figure 7.1   The
decision process

Decision making under conditions of uncertainty has been the subject of numerous treatises by decision theorists, who generally follow the pattern given in Figure 7.1, though their main concern is with strategies and prediction of outcomes and in some cases with the relative merits of various choice criteria. Take, for example, the formulation of Raiffa:[4]

> In very rough terms, the analysis of a decision problem under uncertainty requires that you
>
> 1. list the viable options available to you for gathering information, for experimentation, and for action;
> 2. list the events that may possibly occur;
> 3. arrange in chronological order the information you may acquire and the choices you may make as time goes on;
> 4. decide how well you like the consequences that result from the various courses of action open to you; and
> 5. judge what the chances are that any particular uncertain event will occur.

The relationship between these five steps and some of the steps in the decision process outlined in Figure 7.1 is self evident. Notice that in his step 4 Raiffa leaves the ranking of the consequences of alternative strategies to the decision maker and this is analogous to what is referred to later in this chapter as 'personalistic control'. It is, of course, quite possible that the decision maker has no authority to rank consequences on his own and that the criteria are prescribed for him.

There are several further comments that should be made here about Figure 7.1. First, the term *decision* is identified in many people's minds with what is called here *resolution*, while some would argue that a decision includes the determination of selection criteria as well. Most students of statistical decision theory insist that the prediction of outcomes of events is an indispensable part of the decision activity, and some suggest that the enumeration of strategies is also an integral component of decision making. It will become clear from the following discussion, I hope, that the various steps in the decision process are so interrelated and that each may have such significant implications for others, that it is essential to examine all these steps in order to identify the crucial links in the chain of events that leads to the final selection of a particular course of action.

Secondly, there is a need to distinguish between *rational* and *irrational* resolution. It was Lord Chesterfield who wrote:[5]

> We must not suppose, that because a man is a rational animal, he will, therefore, always act rationally; or, because he has such or such a predominant passion, that he will act invariably and consequentially in the pursuit of it. No; we are complicated machines; and though we have one main-spring that gives motion to the whole, we have an infinity of wheels, which, in their turns, retard, precipitate, and sometimes stop that motion.

Dictionary definitions of the term *rational* ('endowed with reason, sensible, sane, moderate', etc.) are not entirely adequate for our purposes. Churchman discusses the concept of reason at some length and comments that

> perhaps the most predominant in the history of thought has been a definition of reason that has tied it closely to logic. The general idea here is that reason consists of logical and consistent steps that go from first principles to rigidly derived conclusions. The steps satisfy all the requirements that formal logic imposes on the so-called reasoning process.[6]

Churchman is not satisfied with this concept and strongly suggests that 'rationality has to do with goals as well as the means of the attainment of goals' and disagrees with those to whom 'it will seem futile to ascribe rationality to goals, unless the goals are regarded as intermediate means to further goals'.[7] The implication of Churchman's arguments is that questions of ethics and morality cannot be divorced from the concept of rationality, since they are often embedded in the determination of goals, otherwise we can never tell 'what is absolutely right'. The proposition that rationality should be judged in terms of what an individual wishes to attain, that is if his intentions are good he is rational and if they are evil he is irrational, is of course contentious. For the sake of our discussion, however, I propose a more restricted definition of rational behaviour. What I mean by rational resolution is that the decision maker conforms to the selection criterion, namely that if after applying the criterion a course of action A is shown to be superior to B, the decision maker does in fact select A in preference to B. If he does not, then the resolution is *irrational*. Further aspects of rationality in decision making are discussed later.

Thirdly, if the discussion of the decision-making process is confined to rational decisions, it follows that every step in the process described in Figure 7.1 is indispensable and that the steps must proceed in the order specified. Information is essential for analysis and for defining measures of performance; without these preliminaries, no model building related to the real world is possible, and without a model to describe the behaviour of the system that the decision maker is trying to control, no possible course of action (or strategies) can be considered; the prediction of outcomes is meaningless unless it corresponds to a set of possible strategies, and the method for choosing between them may well have to be delayed until the expected outcomes have been listed. The final act, that of resolution, is specified by the criterion of choice.

Each step in this process has as its input the outcome of the preceding steps and in turn it provides an input to the next step. The use that is made of these inputs varies from step to step: all the relevant information, for example, is useful for analysis and for model building, but all the detailed data are rarely needed to define performance measures, and once the model has been constructed it embodies the previous steps to an extent that many information details may be ignored in subsequent steps.

Fourthly, it should be noted that while—for the sake of simplicity—the decision process is depicted in Figure 7.1 as a chain of sequential activities, it very often takes the form of recurrent chains with feedback. Figure 7.2 describes in schematic form the model-building process with feedback. Model building is very similar to proposing a hypothesis in the hypothetico-deductive scientific method. The model describes the interrelationships between variables in the system, it attempts to show cause and effect; in short it is designed to provide a predictive tool, so that the controller of the system can proceed to manipulate the variables under his control in order to achieve some desired objectives. But in structuring a theory any given hypothesis needs to be tested and scrutinised, through the design of new experiments and the collection of fresh information, and a model

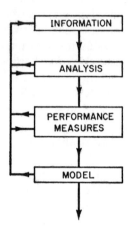

Figure 7.2   Model
building with feedback

constructed as a part of the decision process must be examined in very much the same way. At any stage in this process questions may arise as to the validity of the information, the adequacy of the analysis, the meaning of performance measures, the need for fresh evidence to test the model and some of its implications. This recurrent procedure permeates the decision process.

HOW DATA PROCESSING IMPINGES ON ANALYSIS

The decision process starts with an information input and it is often asserted that information processing that precedes this input is quite distinct from the subsequent analysis that marks the beginning of the decision process proper.

If, however, we examine the activities that are involved in data or information processing on the one hand and in analysis on the other, we find that the line of demarcation is far from being distinct, if it can be drawn at all. Data processing (see Chapter 5): consists of three major activities: data and information storage, data handling and the presentation of information, and these activities may be further divided into several categories, as shown in Figure 7.3.

Let us now turn to analysis. What does the decision maker do when he is engaged in analysis? First, he checks for consistency of the data that he is presented with, and if he detects inconsistencies, he demands an explanation. This activity of *checking for consistency* is not very different from *verifying*, which is part of data handling. Secondly, he arranges the information in a certain sequence and in a form that allows him and his colleagues to comprehend the full import of the information, and this activity of *arranging* is very similar to *sorting* in data handling.

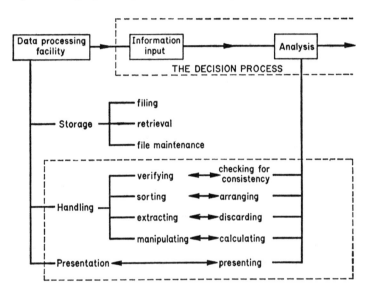

Figure 7.3   Data processing and analysis

The decision maker then discards that information which he considers to be less significant for his analysis than the information that he chooses to retain for further examination, and this is precisely what *extracting* in data handling is designed to do. He then carries out *calculations*, which are akin to *data manipulating* in data handling, and finally he presents the results in a form that is most convenient and useful for the model-building stage.

All these activities, that form a part of what I call 'analysis' (namely, checking data to eliminate inconsistencies, arranging data, discriminating between more significant and less significant information, computing new sets of data and finally summarising and presenting the results), are precisely mirrored by those listed under the heading 'data processing' (except for data storage). Data processing is, therefore, not distinct from analysis; the two greatly overlap.

In fact, if the decision maker were clearly to specify in advance how the information should be handled prior to presentation, then the whole function of analysis could be transferred to the data-processing facility, so that information input to the decision maker is then already presented in a digested and convenient form for him to proceed immediately to the next stages in the decision process, namely to determining performance measures and to constructing a model.

In reality, of course, there are many circumstances in which the whole function of analysis cannot be transferred in this way. First, we find that many decision makers loathe delegating this function and thereby allowing the data processing facility to encroach on their domain of responsibility. Secondly, and this is perhaps fundamentally more important, the decision maker is not always in a position to specify in advance what analysis should be undertaken. As already indicated in the diagram in Figure 7.2, analysis, setting performance measures and model building, are parts of an iterative process. Very often, it is only after an attempt has been made to construct a model and after its weaknesses have been exposed, that the need for further analysis can be realised and a re-evaluation of the specified performance measures can be undertaken.

There is, therefore, a limit to the degree of transfer of the analysis function from the decision maker to the data-processing facility, even when the decision maker genuinely acquiesces in such a move. However, the point is worth making that when model building processes are comparatively routine with a few novel features—and administration in industry and government abounds with such instances—a remarkable slice of the analysis function *can* be transferred from the decision process to data processing and there is a great deal of evidence to suggest that this transfer is accelerated when the data processing facility takes the form of a computer-based information centre.

What must be realised is that even when the computer centre assumes an increasingly important role in the analysis function, the decision maker must retain the responsibility for drawing specifications for the output of the computer centre, not just to ensure that this output is relevant to the subsequent model-building stage, but to underline the maxim that the output should be properly geared to the decision process as a whole. When this does not happen and the computer centre gets out of step, when it starts imposing its own formats of analyses and generates information at the wrong time and the wrong place (from the decision maker's viewpoint), then the computer centre ceases to be an integrated part of the control mechanism and sooner or later the decision maker begins to keep his own records, to carry out some of the missing computations ('missing' from his viewpoint), to rearrange and present data, in short to undertake some of the detailed data processing and analysis that the computer centre has failed or was unwilling to perform.

THE HALLMARKS OF RATIONALITY

It is sensible to analyse the decision process in all its ramifications only against the assumption of rational behaviour on the part of the decision maker. If he behaves irrationally, namely if he does not (when he makes a resolution) abide by an agreed criterion that specifies how a choice is to be made, that much of what is accomplished in the preceding stages of the decision process may be irrelevant or immaterial to his final resolution. Consequently, rationality in this context is best defined by reference to the decision process itself: each time the final resolution deviates from what would be expected from following the process, then the resolution cannot be said to be rational.

The decision maker may argue that though his resolution does not conform to the official decision process, it should still be regarded as rational, because it would not conform if a different decision process is agreed upon, namely a procedure that he approves of. But the question still remains: does he or does he not adhere to this decision process? If he does, that is if it is possible to find another process (which we may conveniently term 'the informal decision process', as opposed to the formal, or official one) then the decision maker acts rationally from his viewpoint, but alas irrationally from the organisation's viewpoint. If, on the other hand, this other decision process has not been clearly specified and is little more than a figment of the decision maker's imagination, then his behaviour is irrational from every viewpoint.

Determination of choice criteria

A distinction must, therefore, be made between the situation where the decision maker has been responsible for, or a party to, the determination of the choice criterion, and the situation where he has not. In the latter, 'rationality' and 'irrationality' must be judged with reference either to the organisation or to the individual decision maker. If he makes a resolution that conforms to the criterion imposed by the organisation, but one that he personally profoundly disagrees with, then from the organisation's viewpoint the resolution is perfectly rational, while from the individual's standpoint is irrational. If he makes a resolution that conforms to his own criterion in opposition to the one specified by the organisation, then the position is reversed. In either case, there is a conflict between the decision maker and the organisation.

If the decision maker is responsible for the criterion of choice, the decision process is *personalistic* in character, namely the resolution at the end of the process becomes a function of the decision maker's own personality, his beliefs, his attitudes and his value judgements. His resolution for given circumstances may well be different from that of another individual, though both may still behave rationally by our definition. If, on the other hand, the decision maker does not participate in the determination of a choice criterion, the decision process is *impersonalistic* and the outcome must be the same for different decision makers, if they all behave rationally.

Some corrolaries of rational choice

If the discussion is confined to rational choice, the following observations can be made about the final resolution by the decision maker.

1. If the decision process produces only one possibility, there can obviously be no free choice exercised by the decision maker, and therefore no decision. The essence of a *decision* is that the decision maker has several possibilities open to him, so that he can exercise the prerogative of a conscious choice.

2. If there are several possibilities and if an agreed criterion allows complete ranking in terms of a composite measure of performance (which incorporates several measures or yardsticks), then the ranking process automatically causes one possibility to be superior to others. If the decision maker behaves rationally, he must select this one. In that sense, therefore, he does not really exercise any free choice; the choice has already been made for him by the ranking criterion. Thus, once a choice criterion is agreed upon, the final resolution, or choice, is *automatic*, and again the decision maker becomes redundant at that stage of the decision process.

3. If ranking is possible and if several possibilities have equal ranking, then the selection criterion fails to discriminate between them. Unless the existing criterion for choice is modified, or a new one is employed, there is no way in which the decision maker can be guided in giving preference, and any choice he makes under such conditions may be regarded as a random choice. Once again, the decision maker is made redundant, since random choices can be made equally well through the use of electro-mechanical devices.

4. If the available information is inadequate, or if the analysis of the information is not penetrating enough, to allow the possible strategies to be ranked at all, then any choice between them can only be made at random, irrespective of how refined and robust the criterion of choice is, and this random choice can as well be made mechanically.

Perhaps the obvious conclusion to be drawn from this discussion is that if a free choice by the decision maker exists at all, it does not lie at the stage called 'resolution' in the decision process, but at the stage where the criterion of choice is determined. If possibilities can be ranked, then for any criterion of choice, resolution is automatic and trivial. The only excuse for including it in the decision process in Figure 7.1 is to provide a landmark to indicate that the process has come to a final conclusion.

Formal and informal procedures

The crux of the decision process lies in the model-building stage and in the determination of the criterion of choice. It is mainly in the context of these two stages in the process that the degree of initiative allowed to the decision maker should be viewed, since these are the significant components in the process that characterise the control mechanism as being formal or informal, personalistic or impersonalistic (see Figure 7.4).

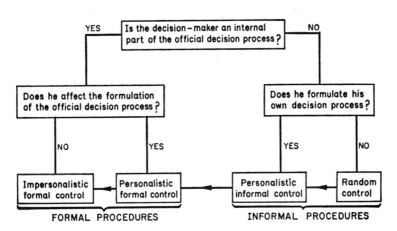

Figure 7.4   Formal and informal procedures

The distinction between personalistic and impersonalistic control is somewhat more complicated than is suggested in this diagram and a more detailed discussion of this problem is given later, but crude as it is, the diagram suggests an interesting hierarchy of four control procedures. Random control is at one extreme end of the scale and impersonalistic-formal control at the other. Observations of the development of control procedures in industry suggest that they have a tendency to move in a direction shown by the arrows: Starting with a situation in which decisions and corrective actions are taken in a haphazard fashion (random control) in the absence of any directives, an individual emerges and tries to regularise these actions and mould them into a systematic and consistent pattern. As long as his procedure does not have the formal blessing of the organisation, it may be characterised as personalistic-informal. Subsequently the procedure is formalised and when eventually it tends to be independent of the individual it becomes impersonalistic-formal. The growth of enterprises from family concerns to large companies, the introduction of computer systems, the aftermath of developing a new product— all these are examples in which the process of formalisation and impersonalisation can very often be detected.

Maximising utility

So far the discussion of rationality has been confined to the final stages of the decision process. But what about the earlier stages? One way of considering a decision maker who is engaged in constructing a model and weighing alternative strategies, is to regard him as a problem solver. When is his behaviour as a problem solver to be regarded as rational? Von Neumann and Morgenstern briefly discuss the concept of rationality in problem solving and say that an individual who attempts to obtain the maximum utility is said to act rationally and this definition is not at variance with the one suggested here. They go on to say:

> But it may safely be stated that there exists, at present, no satisfactory treatment of the question of rational behavior. There may, for example, exist several ways by which to reach the optimum position; they may depend on the knowledge and understanding which the individual has and upon the paths of action open to him.[8]

There may be an implication in this statement that rationality is to be regarded as a function of the method used to arrive at the optimum solution, that if an optimum solution to a problem exists, an individual is said to behave rationally if he arrives at the solution through the use of the best (most efficient?) generally known method. This train of thought would suggest that rationality should be defined in absolute terms, which are determined by the problem and by the general consensus of opinion as to how to solve it, so that if an individual is seen to follow this path, his behaviour is considered to be rational.

This is certainly not the implication that I wish to convey in the definition of rationality suggested here. If an individual fails to follow the generally accepted path because of his ignorance of the existence of this path, and if he persists in following his own path, then from his point of view he behaves perfectly rationally, even if he does not attain the best solution and even if his actions appear to make no sense to a knowledgeable outsider. It seems to me that the first statement of von Neumann and Morgenstern is adequate to describe rationality in the context of this discussion, namely that *an individual is said to behave rationally if he at-tempts to obtain the maximum utility*. Rationality is, therefore, a relative concept. What is utility to one individual (let alone maximum utility) may not be utility to another. In a personalistic type of control the goals, the utilities, the criterion of choice between alternatives and the final result of the decision process, may be very different for different individuals, even though all may behave rationally in the context of the definition given here.

The method of solution

What happens, one might ask, when an individual has followed his own method of solution and refuses to adopt what is generally acknowledged to be a superior method, in other words the individual can no longer argue that he is unaware of the existence of this other method? Does he behave rationally?

The answer, it seems to me, lies in whether the alleged superior method yields a better solution or not. The criterion as to what is 'better' has already been determined and agreed by the individual, prior to, or in the course of, following his own path to arrive at a solution. If a new method is brought to his attention and is shown to produce a better result, better as judged by this criterion, and if the individual persists in ignoring this method, how can he claim to act rationally? In our definition, he no longer attempts to obtain the maximum utility, and therefore he ceases to behave rationally.

If, on the other hand, the new method produces the same or as good a solution as the one derived by the individual's method, then superiority of one method over another can be claimed only on grounds of efficiency (speed of calculations or economy in procedure), rigour, convenience or elegance. And here the answer to the question whether the individual continues to behave rationally depends on whether he accepts these arguments. If he does, yet refuses to change his method, he is irrational; if he does not, his behaviour from his viewpoint continues to be rational, though to others it may seem rather eccentric.

FREEDOM OF CHOICE

The many references to the ability of an individual to make a choice from among a number of possibilities naturally raises the question: how and under what circumstances can an individual be said to have a freedom of choice?

This problem has exercised the minds of philosophers throughout the ages and has been the subject of numerous treatises. Of all the various approaches to this subject I have chosen to discuss briefly three: the first identifies free choice as the absence of compulsion; the second is tied up with the question of determinism; the third is the view of Ofstad, who provides a comprehensive review of the literature on this topic and suggests his own definition of freedom of choice.

Absence of compulsion

It was Aristotle who first discussed 'voluntary' as opposed to 'involuntary' behaviour and many philosophers subsequently adhered to the view that freedom of choice of a course of action should be defined as one that is not subject to external compulsion. Schlick says on this matter:

> Freedom means the opposite of compulsion; a man is free if he does not act under compulsion, and he is compelled or unfree when he is hindered from without in the realization of his natural desires.[9]

Ofstad devotes a short chapter to the discussion of compulsion and starts off by saying.

> It is usual to distinguish between physical and psychical external compulsion. If a man lifts me up and throws me into the ocean against my will, this is called 'physical compulsion'. If he directs me to jump at the point of a pistol, the compulsion is called 'psychical', and if I jump from philosophical conviction, there is no external compulsion at all.[10]

Ofstad then proceeds to discuss physical compulsion, psychical compulsion from without, and inner compulsion and concludes that 'It is impossible to make general statements as to whether man's decisions are free or unfree in any of the senses indicated in this chapter.'[11]

If we were to accept that freedom of choice is manifest in the absence of compulsion, then in the context of business decisions such freedom never exists. In most cases the decision maker is faced with constraints which rule out the choice of many possibilities. Does the fact that the set of *feasible* choices (namely those that are not eliminated by 'compulsion') is necessarily limited deny the decision maker a free choice? If we were to answer 'yes', then it is difficult to conceive of any circumstances in which an individual can have complete freedom of choice. Suppose I am alone on a desert island, free from the vagaries of other people and ostensibly free to do whatever I like. But in terms of a definition that is founded on the absence of compulsion I am not free to go to the theatre, because of the physical constraints imposed by the environment. Similarly, on a desert island or anywhere else, I am not 'free' to decide to sing in an opera, simply because I have no talent in that direction.

It is, therefore, necessary to adopt a more realistic definition that refers to freedom of choice within a *given* environment. Thus, the desert island does not offer a theatre and nature has not endowed me with a talent to sing hence these problems do not arise. Even when physical constraints are ignored and compulsion is defined as resulting from actions taken by other people, it is not difficult to argue that in a business environment such a definition leaves one with very little, if any, freedom of choice. It is more profitable, therefore, to turn one's attention to the set of choices *open* to the decision maker, not those that have been eliminated by external forces. Freedom of choice is then said to exist if an individual has two or more courses of action available to him and if there is no *external compulsion* to make him choose one of them.

There may still remain an inner compulsion to adopt one course of action rather than another, but it seems to me that this matter should not be dealt with as a problem in freedom of choice but as one of rational or irrational behaviour.

Freedom from determinism

Numerous writers over the ages have held that free will exists in the absence of causes that lead an individual to make a particular choice, and this view has generated heated discussions among philosophers on the question of determinism and on whether it is or it is not compatible with the notion of freedom of choice.

Determinism is associated with the notion of causality. Events in the universe are related to others through some general laws of nature and it is therefore arguable whether decisions can be divorced from other events in the universe. The relationship between events or entities is often interpreted as a cause-and-effect mechanism (if entity A assumes a state A_1 then entity B assumes the state B_1), but in viewing a given situation in which certain events have occurred it is sometimes difficult to say which is the cause and which is the effect (has A caused B to become B_1 or has B caused A to be A_1?). Some writers argue that this is an important issue in identifying whether a decision is free or not. This raises the problem of how to identify cause and effect and various criteria have been suggested by a number of writers.

1. *A time-dependent definition.* In the relationship between A and B the former is the cause if a change in the state of A takes place *before* a change in state B. The next step is to define 'before', since a time lag between the two events may not always be discernable.

2. *A one-sided causality definition.* If when the state of A is changed a change in the state of B is observed, but not *vice versa*, then A is said to be the cause in the relationship between A and B.

6

3. *An irreversibility definition.* If entity B moves from state B_1 to state B_2, but cannot move back without the intervention of external forces, then the event that is described by B_2 is the result and not the cause of another event.

The adoption of one of these definitions may or may not affect the existence of freedom of the will from determinism, depending on one's viewpoint. The literature abounds with numerous and detailed discussions to support various propositions, from those who argue that free volition is not caused, to those who believe like Spinoza that the will 'requires a cause by which it may be determined, as in everything else in the universe'.[12]

Ofstad's view

Ofstad discusses freedom from determinism (or 'freedom as indeterminancy', as he puts it) at some length[13] and proceeds to consider four other possible definitions of free will: 'freedom as self-expression', 'freedom as rationality', 'freedom as virtue' and 'freedom as power'. Some of the arguments under these various headings are very closely related to the discussion on determinism, others are covered in my previous discussion of the concepts of rationality and personalistic control and need not concern us any further here. What is, perhaps, more interesting is that after a detailed discourse of free will in relation to ethical criteria, Ofstad concludes with his own definition of a free person:

> P is a *free person* if, and only if, the following three conditions are fulfilled: (1) P's ethical system is oriented towards such values as love, tolerance and human dignity, (2) he has knowledge of his ethical system, his motivation and choice-situations so that he is able to find out which course of action will be best in accordance with this system, and (3) he is so strongly and whole-heartedly disposed to decide in favor of the course of action which he believes to be the right one, that he does not have to make any efforts in order to decide.[14]

This definition is not very satisfactory. The first condition requires definition of love, tolerance and human dignity, and above all it requires a definition of the degrees of orientation towards these values that would allow a person to be identified as free or otherwise. The second condition imposes similar difficulties of definition: what level of intimate knowledge does a person have to possess of his ethical system, motivation and possible strategies to satisfy this condition? And do we ever get a situation where full knowledge of these issues does in fact exist? The first part of condition (3) is reminiscent of what I called personalistic control, but the second part is too ambiguous to be helpful: if the individual does not require to make any effort to make a decision, then the implication is that the outcomes of possible choices have already been ranked and in terms of Figure 7.1 all that is left is to make the final selection, which then—as already pointed out—becomes a trivial component in the decision process.

One implication of Ofstad's definition is that freedom of choice is a matter of degree, and while we have as yet no way of ranking this degree of freedom (except, perhaps, in some trivial cases), the notion of partial freedom may be thought by some to be useful. As Ofstad says in his preface:

> Power to decide is not something which we have either in full or not at all. It is a matter of degrees and individual variations. What one man can do is not necessarily what another can do. What we can do in one situation may be different from what we can accomplish in another.[15]

The other implication of Ofstad's definition, in the context of our discussion process, is that personalistic control does (or may) involve free choice whereas impersonalistic control does not (this is my own interpretation) and this is an implication that I fully endorse. It seems, however, that this result may be obtained by adopting the definition that freedom of choice exists when an individual has two or more courses of action available to him and there is no external compulsion to choose a particular one. This definition avoids many of the difficulties that are presented by a wider concept based on the absence of compulsion (some of these difficulties were discussed earlier) and it ignores the circumstances that have led to delimiting the range of available choices. Admittedly, if two individuals P_1 and P_2 are placed in identical situations and if P_1 is allowed three courses of action and P_2 is allowed only two, then P_1's scope is wider than that of P_2. However, *both individuals are free to make a choice.* Some concept to indicate and even to measure this difference in scope would, therefore, be useful and while I am not proposing to define such a concept here, I suggest that it need not be part of the definition of freedom of choice.

ON UTILITY*

The criterion of choice involves the determination of a measure of utility which incorporates the various entities defined as measures of performance and gives expression to the objectives of the decision process. Take, for example, a production system in which capacity constraints lead to a conflict between several products. If the measures of performance are defined as the profit values for these products, and if the profit for one product can be increased at the expense of that derived from another product, then the purpose of the single utility scale is to take account of all

* This section (pp. 151–157) may be omitted at first reading.

the individual measures of performance, and in the example cited it may simply be the algebraic sum of all the profit values. If the total profit for all the products is defined as the utility function, and thereby implies that the objective of the decision process is to secure as high a value of this function as possible, then the decision maker need no longer consider the effect of possible strategies on any one particular product; the conflict between the products is reconciled by the introduction of the utility scale.

Or take the case of controlling inventory to meet variable demand. If stock is depleted, demand cannot be met and if customers are not prepared to wait until the stock is replenished, then loss of revenue is incurred during the stock runout period, coupled with a loss in customer good-

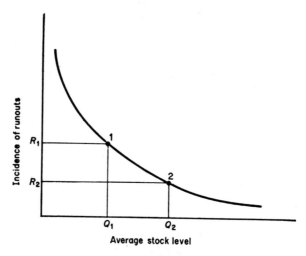

Figure 7.5   Trading-off stock level against stock runout

will. The incidence of runouts (or alternatively, the percentage of the amount of stock not available on demand) can be reduced if the average stock holding is increased. The relationship between these two performance measures is shown in Figure 7.5, where strategy 1 associated with R_1 of runouts requires Q_1 average stock level and is compared with strategy 2, for which the corresponding values are R_2 and Q_2 respectively, and $R_1 > R_2$ but $Q_2 > Q_1$. If both measures can be translated to cost figures, for example by considering linear cost parameters a and b for the two measures respectively (namely a is the cost of increasing runout incidence by one unit and b is the cost of increasing the average stock level by one unit), then the utility function becomes $aR_1 + bQ_1$ for strategy 1 and

$aR_2 + bQ_2$ for strategy 2 and the one that has the lower value (since the implied objective is to minimise the total cost) is preferable.

It may be useful to pause here and state some axioms and corollaries associated with utility theory which are due to von Neumann and Morgenstern.[16]

1. If there are two entities u and v and an individual is asked to state his preference, then only one of three relationships exists:

   $u > v$ which means that he prefers u to v

   $u < v$ which means that he prefers v to u

   $u = v$ which means that he has no preference; both are equally desirable or undesirable.

2. If there are three entities u, v and w and if he states that $u > w$ and $w > v$, then $u > v$. This axiom implies transitivity of preference.

3. A weighting parameter α is defined in the interval $0 < \alpha < 1$. If there are three entities $u > w > v$ then a number α exists such that

$$\alpha u + (1 - \alpha)v = w \tag{1}$$

   i.e. u and v are given complementary weights, such that the decision maker becomes indifferent to the weighted sum or to w.

   Similarly, a value of α exists so that

$$\alpha u + (1 - \alpha)v > w \tag{2}$$

   and a value of α also exists so that

$$\alpha u + (1 - \alpha)v < w \tag{3}$$

   It follows that if there are three entities $u = w = v$, then Equation (1) is true for any value of α.

4. If there are two entities $u > v$ then

$$v > \alpha u + (1 - \alpha)v > u \tag{4}$$

   for any value of α (in the interval 0 to 1).

5. If there are n entities or utilities $u_1, u_2, \ldots, u_n$ such that for any three entities a number α exists to produce a relationship as stated in Equation (1), then the n entities can be arranged in a complete ranking order.

It should, perhaps, be pointed out that in discussing the parameter α von Neumann and Morgenstern often refer to it as a measure of probability. Thus, if there are two possible outcomes to a given course of action and the corresponding utilities of these outcomes are u and v respectively then the expression $\alpha u + (1 - \alpha)v$ states the combination of these two events when α and $(1 - \alpha)$ are their respective probabilities. This combination describes the *expected utility* of the two possible events and, as we shall see later, allows for different strategies to be compared when each strategy may result in one of several outcomes and when each outcome has a single utility. By not specifically stating that α is a measure of probability, it is possible to extend these considerations to the case where each outcome or event has several utilities associated with it.

Let us now examine the way in which such a theory of utility can be applied for single and multiple objectives in deterministic and probabilistic systems.

1. Deterministic outcomes with a single objective

Suppose that a decision maker has m strategies to choose from and a single measure of performance has been defined. If we consider for a moment a deterministic system, so that the utility (described by the measure of performance) or the outcome for each strategy is known, then the decision maker's task is reduced to identifying the highest utility from an array of m values (each corresponding to one of the strategies), and as the theory of utility assumes that complete ranking is possible, there is no difficulty here.

2. Deterministic outcomes with multiple objectives

What we often encounter in reality is the existence of multiple objectives, as we have seen from the few examples cited earlier. Let us confine our discussion to the deterministic cases and consider a set of N measures of performance that are assigned to each course of action. For any given strategy there are N utilities $u_1, u_2, \ldots, u_N$ that describe the corresponding outcome.

The result of arranging N utilities $u_1, u_2, \ldots, u_N$ in a complete ranking order and the computation of weighting parameters, such as α in Equation (1), is to produce a set of weighting constants $a_1, a_2, \ldots, a_N$ so that the composite utility U becomes the weighted sum of the N utilities

$$U = a_1 u_1 + a_2 u_2 + \cdots + a_N u_N \tag{5}$$

If this utility function U is computed for all the available strategies, the results for U can be arranged in a complete ranking order and the best strategy is then immediately identified. This is shown in Table 7.1 which consists of m rows for m possible strategies; each row lists N utilities for any one strategy, so that u_{ij} is the utility j for performance measure j, and the composite utility U_i for strategy i is given in the last column. The values of U_i are related to one composite numerical scale and the one with the highest value signifies the best strategy that should be selected.

TABLE 7.1 A utility table

Measures of performance	Weights	1 a_1	2 a_2	... ...	j a_j	N a_N	Composite utility
Strategies	1	u_{11}	u_{12}		u_{1j}	u_{1N}	U_1
	$\vdots$ i $\vdots$	...			u_{ij}		U_i
	m	...				u_{mN}	U_m

3. Probabilistic outcomes with a single objective

The discussion has so far been confined to decision making under conditions of certainty, namely each strategy is assumed to be associated with a particular outcome. If only a single measure of performance applies, then strategies are automatically ordered; if several measures of performance have to be considered, the ordering is done according to Equation (5) and Table 7.1.

What happens under conditions of risk, when the outcome of any particular strategy is associated with a known probability? It is not difficult to see that composite utilities can be constructed in a similar way. Take first the case of a single measure of performance, so that u_j is the utility of outcome j. In Table 7.2 there are m strategies and n outcomes and the probability matrix p_{ij} is the probability that strategy i will lead to outcome j.

TABLE 7.2 Probability matrix for a single measure of performance

Outcomes Utility		1 u_1	2 u_2	... ...	j u_j	... ...	n u_n	Total prob.	Expected utility
Strategies	1	p_{11}	p_{12}		p_{1j}		p_{1n}	1	U_1
	$\vdots$ i $\vdots$	...			p_{ij}		...	1	U_i
	m	...					p_{mn}	1	U_m

The expected utility from strategy 1 is

$$U_1 = p_{11}u_1 + p_{12}u_2 + \cdots + p_{1j}u_j + \cdots + p_{1n}u_n \qquad (6)$$

where $$p_{11} + p_{12} + \cdots + p_{1j} + \cdots + p_{1n} = 1$$

and similarly the expected utility for each of the m strategies can be found. There is a certain analogy between Table 7.1 and Table 7.2 and between Equations (5) and (6). In view of the axioms enumerated earlier, the values of U_i can be ordered and the optimal strategy can therefore be identified immediately.

4. Probabilistic outcomes with multiple objectives·

The case of multi-performance measures is handled in the following way. First a utility matrix is constructed similar to Table 7.1.

TABLE 7.3   The case of multi-performance measures under conditions of risk

Outcomes		I	j	n		Weights
Measures of performance	I ⋮ k ⋮ N		u_{kj}			a_1 ⋮ a_k ⋮ a_N
Composite utility		u_1	u_j	u_n		

Outcomes Composite utility		I u_1	j u_j	n u_n	Total	Expected utility
Strategies	I ⋮ i ⋮ m		p_{ij}		I I I	U_1 ⋮ U_i ⋮ U_m

Composite utilities are then calculated for the various outcomes and these are used as the utility values in Table 7.2, from which the expected utilities for the available strategies are computed. The procedure is summarised in Table 7.3, in which, for convenience of presentation, the top part is an inverted version of Table 7.1 (i.e. now each column enumerates the utilities for the corresponding outcome) and the bottom part duplicates Table 7.2.

The notion of probability

Circumstances of risk are characterised by the fact that the matrix of decisions and outcomes has occurred many times in the past and that the general pattern of events suggests that steady state conditions prevail to allow an inference for future outcomes to be based on frequencies of past events. But such conditions rarely exist in a business environment, where decisions have to be made under conditions of uncertainty rather than risk, namely where probabilities of future outcomes cannot be equated with frequencies of past outcomes, either because such information is too meagre or non-existent, or because present and future circumstances are believed to be significantly different from the past.

Diverse and often conflicting views are found among decision theorists on how to handle decision making under such conditions. Some suggest methods for determining subjective probability measures, with which the problem of uncertainty can then be handled as if conditions of known risk prevail. Others argue that the conventional concept of probability be abandoned and that other procedures should be employed in order to compare the relative merit of outcomes and hence to identify the most desirable strategy. A fairly detailed account of the various schools of thought on this subject is given by Fishburn[17] and this is not an appropriate place to elaborate on the subject, except to draw attention to the fact that fundamental differences in points of view are very much in existence.

It should perhaps also be pointed out that the very issue of whether a given situation may be described as one of risk or uncertainty is also often open to judgement and dispute. When it comes to making inferences about the future, historical records may well be interpreted in several ways, let alone the challenge that may be levelled at the assertion that such inference is not at all valid. What seems to one individual a perfectly legitimate case of decision under risk may be argued by another as being a case of uncertainty, and the case of uncertainty is then amenable to interpretation in several ways, depending on the individual's school of thought.

THE RELATION BETWEEN UTILITY THEORY AND RATIONALITY

To summarise for the purpose of this discussion; the significant assumptions in the theory of utility suggested by von Neumann and Morgenstern are as follows.

1. An individual is capable of ranking utilities. This assumption also implies consistency, or the need to avoid contradiction: if he prefers u to v then he cannot at the same time prefer v to u or be indifferent as to which utility he prefers.
2. There is transitivity of preference.

3. Weighting factors can be determined to compare utilities and hence to establish a composite utility scale.

It is worthwhile repeating these assumptions because of the significance that has been attributed to these axioms in relation to the concept of rationality. Von Neumann and Morgenstern lay great emphasis on the need for quantitative measurements in economics and after discussing their proposed axioms state that their purpose is 'to find the mathematically complete principles which define "rational behavior" for the participants in a social economy, and to derive from them the general characteristics of that behavior'.[18] Many decision theorists go further and specifically identify the axioms of utility theory as axioms of rational behaviour.

By this test most real decisions will probably have to be regarded as irrational. Take, for example, the assumption that by assigning appropriate weights a multi-objective array can be transformed to a single measure on a composite utility scale. Individuals may have very strong views about the desirability of attaining each of the stated objectives, but may find it impossible to compare and reconcile them.

When, in *As You Like It*, Corin asked Touchstone 'and how like you this shepherd's life?', Touchstone replied:

> Truly shepherd, in respect of itself, it is a good life; but in respect that it is a shepherd's life, it is naught. In respect that it is solitary, I like it very well: but in respect that it is private, it is a very vile life. Now in respect it is in the fields, it pleaseth me well: but in respect it is not in the Court, it is tedious. As it is a spare life (look you) it fits my humour well: but as there is no more plenty in it, it goes much against my stomach. Hast any philosophy in thee shepherd?[19]

In terms of any one objective an individual may find it possible to rank alternatives without much difficulty, but when it comes to declaring how much he is prepared to trade off one utility against another, he may be quite helpless.

Or suppose, for the sake of argument, that a man is faced with the prospect of enjoying the company of one of three ladies, *A*, *B* or *C*. He can enumerate many of the qualities of these splendid ladies—their physical dimensions, the complexion of their skins, the colour of their eyes, their I.Q.'s, the number of pimples per square inch, etc.—but he finds it impossible to come up with a composite measure of utility. The whole idea of a trade-off between any two qualities he finds totally unacceptable. How is he to equate the level of intellect with the density of pimples, he asks? The utility of any one quality may well depend on the presence of other qualities. For example, he may regard a high density of pimples a positive asset when accompanied with certain skin and hair colouring, but a liability in other combinations. Nevertheless, he feels that he can compare two ladies at a time on the basis of an overall evaluation. If, having done this, he states that he prefers A to B and B to C and C to A, he does not abide by the axiom of transitivity of preference. The violation of this axiom undermines the elegant mathematical structure of utility theory and many decision theorists have no patience for such an individual and would simply regard him as irrational.

It should perhaps be pointed out that a 'circular' ranking, such as the one just described, does not necessarily violate the axiom of consistency. Our man may be perfectly consistent in always preferring (within a given space of time) A to B, etc., and avoiding any contradiction between any of two of his statements. Admittedly, faced with a set of preferences as stated so far, he is unable to make a choice, since for any choice that he makes, a better one (as judged by his own preferences) can.be pointed out. Does the fact that he cannot act prove that he is irrational? In our discussion we have drawn a distinction between the determination of choice criteria and the act of selecting between alternatives; our man can argue that he truly *attempts to obtain the maximum utility* (which is our definition of rational behaviour), but the choice criteria do not provide him with a means of making a final selection.

To base a concept of rationality on the axioms of utility theory that were listed earlier is therefore to take a rather narrow view and to exclude from the realm of rationality a significant proportion of decisions that do take place in daily life.

Let us now return to further considerations of personalistic control.

PERSONALISTIC AND IMPERSONALISTIC CONTROL

A distinction was made in Figure 7.4 between personalistic and impersonalistic control by examining whether an individual does or does not affect the formulation of the decision process. In the light of the foregoing discussion it would appear that personalistic and impersonalistic control are not two entirely mutually exclusive categories, but that several shades and degrees of personalistic involvement in the decision process can be identified. Consider the following two groups of questions about an individual:

Group (a): First order of personalistic involvement
  1. Does the individual set up the number and identity of the measures of performance?

2. In case of multi-objectives, does he specify the weighting coefficients that determine the composite utility function? If this is not possible, does he rank the outcomes and does he determine the criterion of choice?
3. Does he specify the array of available strategies?
4. Does he specify the array of possible outcomes?
5. Does he specify whether the decision making process does or does not take place under conditions of certainty?

Group (b): Second order of personalistic involvement (when the decision is not under conditions of certainty)

6. Does he specify which decision theory to apply?
7. If probabilities of possible outcomes are required for the decision process, does he determine their values?
8. Does he determine the value of any subjective parameters (other than probabilities) that may be required in the application of a given decision theory (e.g. the coefficient of optimism if the Hurwicz criterion is adopted)?

Group (a) consists of questions that may be posed for every decision process. Group (b) is only relevant if the decision process is not subject to conditions of certainty.

There are four possible answers to each of these eight questions:

Yes—where the individual does carry out the activity described in the question, and even if his specification may subsequently be modified in the light of criticisms and suggestions by other people, these modifications are comparatively slight or the responsibility for the final specifications clearly lies with the individual.

No—when the specifications described by the question are laid down or are the responsibility of someone else, or when they are covered by standing orders and procedures.

Participates—when the individual is a member of a group of people responsible for the activity described in the question (e.g. when the group is a committee, or when specifications are based on averages of values suggested by several individuals).

Irrelevant—when the question does not apply (any one or several of questions 2, 6, 7 and 8 may become irrelevant in the light of answers to the other questions).

It should be emphasised that answers to the eight questions are to some extent a matter of subjective interpretation on the part of the questioner or investigator. It may be difficult in some circumstances to determine whether an individual should give the first or the third answer to a particular question. Nevertheless, the purpose of these questions is not to compute a crisp numerical value for the level of personalistic involvement of a particular individual, but to produce a profile of his involvement, as demonstrated by the answers in the example shown below (pertaining to a given task or decision process):

Question	Answer		
1	N		
2	P		
3	Y	Legend:	Y—yes
4	Y		N—no
5	N		P—participates
6	N		— —question irrelevant
7	P		
8	—		

If answers to relevant questions are all 'no', then control is strictly formal and impersonalistic, if all the answers are 'yes' then control is purely personalistic, and between these two extremes there is a whole spectrum of combinations.

It is in this context that the tendency of a decision process to become formal and impersonalistic in character may be traced: if answers to the eight questions are monitored over a period of time, then this tendency can be documented, as in the example below:

Question	Time →			
1	N	N	N	N
2	P	N	N	N
3	Y	Y	N	N
4	Y	Y	Y	P
5	N	N	N	N
6	N	N	N	N
7	P	P	N	N
8	—	—	—	—

Where does the decision lie?

Having examined the various stages of the decision process, we may now return to Figure 7.1 and ask: where are the crucial points in this process? Where can the decision maker be said to affect the turn of events?

The answer lies in the degree of personalistic control that he retains. We have already seen how a data-processing facility can encroach on the decision maker's domain by taking over parts or the whole function of analysis. Similarly, when the decision process as a whole becomes more and more impersonalistic, it simply follows the rules, and the rules are sufficiently detailed to cater for an ever increasing number of contingencies, to obliterate the effect of the individual decision maker. In extreme cases, when control is completely impersonalistic, the decision maker ceases to have a meaningful role; he ceases to be a decision maker.

REFERENCES

1. Fishburn, P. C. (1964) *Decision and value theory*, Wiley, p. 11.
2. Ofstad, H. (1961) *An inquiry into the freedom of decision*, Allen and Unwin, p. 15.
3. Churchman, C. W. (1968) *Challenge to reason*, McGraw-Hill, p. 17.
4. Raiffa, H. (1968) *Decision analysis*, Addison Wesley, pp. ix–x.
5. Lord Chesterfield *Letters to his son* (1928), Dent and Sons, London, p. 141.
6. Churchman, C. W., *op. cit.*, p. 95.
7. *Ibid.*, pp. 102, 121.
8. Von Neumann, J. and Morgenstern, O. (1953) *Theory of games and economic behavior*, Princeton University Press, p. 9.
9. Schlick, M. (trans. 1939) *Problems of ethics*, translated by D. Rynin, Dover, p. 150.
10. Ofstad, H., *op. cit.*, p. 37.
11. *Ibid.*, p. 41.
12. Wild, J. (ed. 1930) *Spinoza selections*, The Modern Student's Library, proposition 32.
13. Ofstad, H., *op. cit.*, Chapter III.
14. *Ibid.*, pp. 305–6.
15. *Ibid.*, p. ix.
16. Von Neumann, J. and Morgenstern, O., *op. cit.*, Chapter 3.
17. Fishburn, P. C., *op. cit.*, Chapter 5.
18. Von Neumann, J. and Morgenstern, O., *op. cit.*, p. 31.
19. Shakespeare, W. (1623) *As you like it*, Act 3, Scene 3.

8 Prescription in Management Decisions

Delegation of authority and responsibility is considered one of the fundamental problems in management control. If there is no delegation from one echelon of management to a lower echelon, then the latter is constrained; it cannot exercise any discretion, it cannot meaningfully develop initiative or skill in handling situations which call for managerial intervention, and it cannot, therefore, share in any responsibility for the success or failure of such intervention. The lower echelon may still be useful for monitoring events or as a convenient means of transmitting messages through the system, but it has no active participatory role in the decision process. At the other end of the scale, if complete delegation is practised, the higher management level becomes insipid; full authority and responsibility for decisions are then vested with the lower echelon, and the function and the very existence of the higher level may be put into question.

That some delegation is necessary is therefore obvious enough, if a balance of power and coexistence is to be preserved, and the important question 'how much delegation?' is closely related to the way in which the lower level can be constrained. Three forms of constraining are discussed in this paper.

1. *Prescription for courses of action*—for given circumstances the lower management echelon is told precisely how to act.
2. *Prescription for search-for-solution*—a precise definition of a particular course of action is not given, but the way in which the lower echelon should proceed in determining a desirable course of action within a given framework of constraints is prescribed.
3. *Definition of constraints*—a search-for-solution method is not prescribed and any course of action may be adopted, provided certain objectives and constraints are observed.

The last two forms involve the definition of constraints, which mainly relate to the latitude allowed in utilising resources, but other constraints may also be imposed. The difference between (1) and (3) is that in (2) the lower management echelon must follow certain given procedures in order to arrive at a solution, whereas in (3) there is more 'freedom in scanning and evaluating alternative courses of action, although this freedom may obviously depend on how liberal the constraints are; if they are too rigidly and narrowly defined, this freedom of choice may well be illusory. In (1) no constraints need be defined, because the solution to any given problem that the lower echelon is likely to be confronted with is fully prespecified.

Delegation may therefore be described in terms of these constraining methods in relation to the tasks that the lower echelon is supposed to perform. The more prescriptions of forms (1) and (2) the less delegation of authority to make decisions is to be found, the looser the constraints in form (3), the more freedom of action that the lower echelon can enjoy. Constraining need not, of course, be confined to one of these forms, but may well be a combination of all three, each being applied in different degrees to various arrays of problems that may demand attention and action.

THE MEANING OF PRESCRIPTION

Prescription may be regarded as a set of instructions, imposed by higher management or self imposed, which precisely define how to act in a given set of circumstances. Thus, *prescriptive control* follows a rule book, in which the appropriate courses of action and when they apply are clearly laid down, as opposed to *personalistic control*, which is left to the discretion of the individual. A distinction between two types of prescriptive control may also be useful:

> *Formal*—when search-for-solution or decision follows a specified rule book, recognised by higher management as stating the official procedures to be followed.
>
> *Informal*—when there is no rule book, yet precedent and perhaps tradition dictate what can and what cannot be done, leaving the controller with little room for manoeuvre, though the procedures are not regarded by higher management as binding.

Informal procedures evolve with time; they may represent the results of long experience of tackling problems which might occur and for which no formal procedures exist; they may reflect the informal organisation structure and information flows that have developed over a period of time; or they may be the result of conscious bargaining between members of the organisation at the lower level regarding the demarcation of duties and responsibilities. Formal and informal procedures may be equally prescriptive, they may equally limit discretion and personal choice, but the first is imposed from above, while the latter is self imposed.

This distinction may have a bearing on the effectiveness with which the lower echelon may extract concessions or relaxation of constraints from the higher echelon, presumably because the higher echelon feels more responsible for any detrimental effects of formal prescriptions than for those that result from informal procedures, and because the lower echelon cannot entirely justify militancy as a result of prescriptions that are voluntarily undertaken. This is why higher management, being fully aware of informal control procedures, does not necessarily hasten to formalise them. Apart from the technical problems inherent in formalising procedures, problems that systems analysts are so familiar with (such as sheer mistakes in interpreting existing procedures, dangers of omission, introducing inconsistencies, creating time lags in response, and so on), the risk of formalisation is that it may encourage reactions from the lower echelon, reactions that the higher echelon may consider undesirable.

Examples

What constitutes a prescription? A prescriptive course of action, or a prescriptive search-for-solution procedure, is one that is predetermined and identified by a prespecified set of conditions. These conditions may be event triggered, time triggered, or both.* Here are some examples.

    1. Repair instructions for running a vehicle fleet: 'Institute an engine overhaul when a vehicle
    (a) consumes oil at a rate of 1 quart or more/200 miles, or
    (b) has covered 50 000 miles since its last overhaul, or
    (c) has been in service for four years since its last overhaul.'

Conditions (a) and (b) are event triggered, condition (c) is time triggered. If one of these conditions is satisfied, the man responsible for operating this vehicle knows precisely what to do. Notice that this is not a comprehensive prescription: it does not specify what should be done under other conditions, and this is left to the discretion of the manager of the fleet. Under certain conditions other than those specified he may decide that an overhaul is justified.

    2. As in 1 but add—'Permission for an overhaul under other conditions must be sought from executive A by filling form 12z'. Here no discretion for overhauling engines is retained by the manager of the fleet.

    3. An inventory control policy—'Review the stock level at regular time intervals T and only if the stock level is below s put in a replenishment order to bring the stock level up to S'.

* As in the case of information, see Chapter 5.

Two actions are specified here:

Action	Initiative
(a) Review every period T	time triggered
(b) Replenish stock	$\begin{cases} \text{time triggered by (a)} \\ \text{and event triggered} \end{cases}$

The second action is governed by two conditions: that the reviews should be confined to times T, $2T$, $3T$, ..., and that the stock level is below a predetermined amount s. The first is time triggered and the second is event triggered. Both need to be satisfied for a replenishment order to be released, and no discretion is allowed.

4. Instructions to an insurance broker: 'If the applicant
    (a) is over 25 but under 70 years of age, and
    (b) has not been involved in an accident, and
    (c) wants to insure a car which is not classified as a sports car (see schedule L),

then he may be insured to cover risks listed in schedule M at the following premiums

   x_1 if the car value is below X
   x_2 if the car value is X or above

Drivers aged 20–25 may be insured at 30% above these premiums. Sports cars (schedule L) are acceptable for insurance *provided* their engine capacity does *not* exceed 2500 cc. and the premium is then 50% above the basic rates. Drivers under 20 or over 70 should not be accepted'.

   This set of instructions is based on four characteristics: age, previous accidents, type of car, value of car. Each characteristic consists of several categories as shown below:

Characteristic	Categories
Age	below 20
	20–25
	25–70
	above 70
Previous accidents	0
	above 0
Type of car	$L\begin{cases} L_1 \\ L_2 \end{cases}$
	not L
Value of car	below X
	X or above

These instructions can be summarised in what is called a *decision table* (perhaps a more appropriate name would be a *prescription table*) in Table 8.1, in which twelve cases are listed, each of the first eleven referring to a set of conditions mentioned in the instruction schedule. The type of car is designated as either L or not L, and when it belongs to class L it is classified as either L_1 (2500 cc. or below) or L_2 (above 2500 cc.).

TABLE 8.1   Decision table for example 4

Case	Conditions				Prescription
	(a) Age	(b) Previous accidents	(c) Type of car	(d) Value of car	Level of premium
1	< 20				NO (1)
2	> 70				NO (1)
3			L_2		NO (1)
4	25–70	0	not L	< X	x_1 (2)
5	25–70	0	not L	≥ X	x_2 (2)
6	25–70	0	L_1	< X	$1·5x_1$ (2)
7	25–70	0	L_1	≥ X	$1·5x_2$ (2)
8	20–25	0	not L	< X	$1·3x_1$ (2)
9	20–25	0	not L	≥ X	$1·3x_2$ (2)
10	20–25	0	L_1	< X	$1·8x_1$ (2)
11	20–25	0	L_1	≥ X	$1·8x_2$ (2)
12	20–70	> 0	not L_2		?

Notes: (1) mandatory; (2) permissive.

Notice that cases 4–11 may be described as *permissive* ('... he may be insured'); an applicant may fall into one of the categories 4–11, but the insurance broker is not obliged by the instructions to accept him. Cases 1–3 are mandatory; an applicant in these categories is not acceptable. Prescription in case 12 is *unspecified*. It is not clear what the insurance broker is expected to do when he is faced with an applicant in this category; he may either refer such cases to head office, or he may wish to exercise discretion (in which case one would hope that he would have enough sense not to offer terms which are more favourable than under cases 4–11).

It is not difficult to see that the other examples cited earlier may also be presented in the form of similar decision tables, in which the various contingencies are listed and the corresponding actions specified.

5. A double sampling plan in quality control: 'Take a sample n from a batch; accept the batch if you find less than c_1 defectives, reject it if

you find more than c_2 (where $c_2 > c_1$). If the number of defectives is between c_1 and c_2, take a second sample. Accept the batch if the total number of defectives in both samples is below c_3, otherwise reject the batch.'

This plan can be presented in a graphical form (Figure 8.1), by a flow diagram (Figure 8.2), or in a decision table (Table 8.2).

TABLE 8.2   Decision table for example 5

Case	Conditions		Prescription
	(a) Sample size	(b) No. defective	
1	n	$< c_1$	accept
2	n	$> c_2$	reject
3	n	c_1 to c_2	{take second sample go to 4, 5
4	$2n$	$< c_3$	accept
5	$2n$	$\geq c_3$	reject

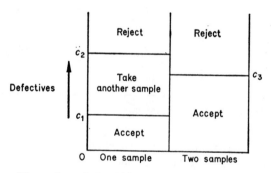

Figure 8.1   A double sampling plan (example 5)

TYPES OF INSTRUCTIONS

These examples should be sufficient to illustrate that all prescriptions can be presented in decision tables, and also that there are different categories in which instructions can be classified:

1. *mandatory*—the course of action is clear; no room for manoeuvre.
2. *permissive*—if the conditions apply, the decision maker may or may not wish to take action; if he decides to pursue, the course of action is laid down.
3. *discretionary*—as 'permissive', but instead of a single specified course of action, latitude is given as to what action is most appropriate.

4. *unspecified*—none of the sets of conditions in the decision table strictly applies; the decision maker has two choices:
   (a) appeal for guidance
   (b) interpret the case as best he can (probably in the spirit of other cases specified in the table) in terms of whether action is called for and what form it should take.

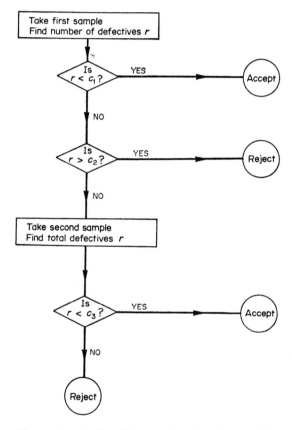

Figure 8.2   A flow diagram for a double sampling
plan (example 5)

The term 'discretionary'* for category (3) is perhaps not entirely satisfactory, because there is a certain amount of discretion in (2) and (4), though of a different kind. In (2) discretion is exercised as to whether to

* Discretion—liberty of decision as one thinks fit, absolutely or within limits (*The Concise Oxford Dictionary*, 1964).

apply the decision table, whereas in (3) the area of discretion is much wider. In (4) too, discretion is involved, often through oversight, sometimes by design, but in neither case is it officially incorporated in the control system as in (2) and (3).

Clearly, a set of instructions does not necessarily fall into one of these categories to the exclusion of the others. The examples 1 and 4 (pp. 165–6) have mandatory and permissive ingredients whereas examples 2, 3 and 5 have mandatory instructions. The more frequently a decision maker finds that he has to apply mandatory instructions, the more formally prescriptive the control is; the more frequently he encounters permissive, discretionary or unspecified instructions, the more personal (unless it is informally prescriptive) it is. Thus prescription is a matter of degree, perhaps best measured by the relative frequencies with which the four categories apply when cases which are encountered in practice are referred to the decision table.

Prescriptions which are ingredients of decision tables are related to courses of action. Let us now turn to decision making under constraints, for which the well known allocation model would be a useful starting point.

ALLOCATION OF RESOURCES

Decision making under constraints has become a concept that most students of management are familiar with. A constraint is a limitation, which defines a condition or a set of conditions that must be satisfied for a decision to be valid; so long as the constraint is not violated, the decision maker has a freedom of choice, and within the framework of the possibilities open to him, a management scientist strives to identify the one that he should select, so as to optimise the outcome by some predetermined criteria.

Take the following formulation of an allocation problem by a linear programming model. Suppose there are m resources with which n products need to be produced and the manager is required to determine the product-mix, namely the amount of each product. The OR (operational research) analyst visualises an allocation matrix as in Table 8.3. The entries in the table signify the result of the allocation decision: x_j is the quantity of product j, requiring a_{1j} units of capacity of resource 1, a_{2j} of resource 2, and so on. Thus, each row in the matrix prescribes the inputs needed of each given resource (say, row i for resource i) for the n products. The last row is the payoff (for example, the profit) for each unit of product, namely c_1 is the payoff per unit of product 1, c_2 for product 2, and so on. The column on the extreme right expresses the capacity constraints, A_1 being the maximum capacity available for resource 1, A_i for resource i, etc.

TABLE 8.3   An allocation matrix

Resources		x_1	x_2	...	x_j	...	x_n	Maximum capacity constraints
		Product quantities						
	1	a_{11}	a_{12}	...	a_{1j}	...	a_{1n}	A_1
	$\vdots$							$\vdots$
	i	a_{i1}	a_{i2}	...	a_{ij}	...	a_{in}	A_i
	$\vdots$							
	m							A_m
Payoffs		c_1	c_2		c_j		c_n	

Now, the payoff derived from producing x_1 units of product 1 is $c_1 x_1$, so that the total payoff for all n products is

$$Z = c_1 x_1 + c_2 x_2 + \cdots + c_n x_n \qquad (1)$$

But in determining the amounts $x_1, x_2, \ldots$ the decision maker must not violate the capacity constraints. If it takes a_{11} units of resource 1 to produce a unit of product 1 then x_1 units will require $a_{11}x_1$; similarly x_2 units of product 2 will involve $a_{12}x_2$, and so on. The total requirement of resource 1 then becomes $a_{11}x_1 + a_{12}x_2 + \cdots + a_{1n}x_n$. To ensure that the maximum capacity constraint A_1 is not violated, the decision maker needs to comply with the condition

$$a_{11}x_1 + a_{12}x_2 + \cdots + a_{1n}x_n \leq A_1 \qquad (2)$$

Similarly, for resource i the constraint is

$$a_{i1}x_1 + a_{i2}x_2 + \cdots + a_{in}x_n \leq A_i \qquad (3)$$

and there are m such constraints.

The OR (operational research) formulation of this allocation problem then becomes: find the quantities x_j so that the objective function (1) is minimum, subject to the m constraints defined in (2) and (3). Computational procedures are available to determine the solution to this problem, so that once the objective function and the constraints are defined, the procedures can be followed and the corresponding solution is duly arrived at.

THE PLANNING PROCESS

Most readers will be familiar with this model. The purpose of describing it here is to use it as an illustration of the model building process that is involved in any management planning task, which in essence consists of scheduling future activities and allocation of resources: allocation to departments, allocation to products or plants, allocation to future time periods.

It is not suggested, of course, that all allocation problems can be reduced to a linear programming formulation with a simple objective function as described in Equation (1), but the model-building process of all planning activities comprises essentially the same three stages: first, define the problem and the aims of the exercise (i.e. construct an objective function); secondly, enumerate the means and their limitations (i.e. define the resources and their constraints); thirdly, determine which course of action should be selected (i.e. find the optimal solution).

Each of these three ingredients (which may be succinctly described as *aims, means* and *solution*) has a different significance at different levels in the management hierarchy. The higher echelons are mainly concerned with aims and means. They define explicitly or implicitly the objectives of the organisation and its parts, and they also define, with varying degrees of detail, the means and their constraints. As instructions filter down the management hierarchy, these definitions are progressively interpreted and constraints become more closely defined. And because each echelon prescribes narrower constraints to the lower echelon, the room for manoeuvre and the degree of discretion that the lower echelon can exercise diminish accordingly.

SEARCH FOR SOLUTIONS

Take the example of an allocation problem that can be described by a linear programming model, such as the one discussed earlier. If a decision maker is charged with the solution of this problem after the model has been set for a given objective function and a given set of constraints that are defined by his superiors—what room for manoeuvre does he have? What initiative can he demonstrate? The answer is 'virtually none'. Even if there are many possibilities that can be enumerated, there is only one optimal solution, only one that will yield the best results as viewed by the objective function. Even the process of scanning the feasible possibilities in order to identify the optimal one is laid down by efficient search procedures, so that the decision maker is no longer in a position of having to make a conscious choice after a close examination of the possibilities that are 'open' to him; these possibilities are not really open at all. He is not even in a position to demonstrate excellence in conducting his search. The choice is made for him, by defining in an unequivocal manner the way in which the evaluation of choices is to be carried out and how the choice that is superior to others is to be identified. In short, he is no longer a decision maker; he becomes a mere technician, whose function is to ensure that procedures are faithfully followed and that the data input is free from errors in the course of transfer.[1]

But if a search procedure for finding the optimal solution is not laid down, either because such procedures do not exist, or simply because management is unaware of available methods for solving the problems under consideration, then an area of discretion in determining the solution can be maintained, even when the parameters of aims and means are defined. In either case, the decision maker is left to his own devices to design and conduct his own search, and the likelihood of him finding the optimal solution (if one exists) would depend on his skill and experience, on his intuitive flair, and on the complexity of the problem. Sometimes he would develop heuristic methods of solution, which eventually reach the stage where they can be systematised and formalised, and as soon as this is accomplished, the area of discretion again contracts or vanishes, depending on the degree of prescription that the formalised search method assumes.

Thus, the rate at which the area of discretion contracts reflects the extent to which management is prescription minded. Neither the ignorance of existing methods, nor the non-availability of methods, will deter a resolute management from prescribing search procedures or even final solutions in an authoritarian fashion, although the chances are that if the manager can show time and time again that he can produce better solutions, such authoritarian prescriptions are bound to erode. When the prescriptions are based, however, on known efficient search procedures, particularly when they yield optimal or near-optimal solutions, then the manager is less likely to improve on these methods and they are less likely to be discredited.

When management is not prescription minded, and is even anxious to preserve an area of discretion at the search-for-solution stage, then it may attempt to extend this policy to situations for which efficient search methods for optimal solutions do exist, although the discrepancies between solutions that the manager will come up with and the optimal solutions are bound to provide effective ammunition to those (often including OR practitioners) who strongly advocate that prescriptive methods of solutions should be adopted. In addition, the constant pressure of competition may strengthen the case for prescriptive methods, when they can be shown to be effective, and particularly when competitors are known to use such methods successfully. It is therefore not surprising that tools of management science have been increasingly in demand, from work study and Taylor's methods at the beginning of the century to OR and computer techniques in more recent years.

The conclusion must be drawn that as management science progresses and as better and more refined tools for comparing courses of action are devised, yielding optimal and near-optimal solutions, the tendency for more prescription for this stage of the model building process is bound to grow. And this tendency can only lead to an increasing amount of programmed decisions, which Simon described as well-structured, routine and repetitive,[2] the kind of decisions to which operational research techniques and computer processing methods have made many contributions in the past decade.

MEANS

The less discretion managers have at the search-for-solution stage, the more pressure they will exert to participate in the earlier stage (that concerned with definition of means and constraints). This tendency is already becoming apparent from observations of the effects of introducing computer systems and OR techniques to industrial organisations. And this tendency is natural enough. Having prescribed how an allocation problem can be solved, the manager (aided and abetted by the OR man) turns his attention to aims and means and begins to question them, and his immediate target is naturally the specified constraints: What do they mean? Under what circumstances can they be violated and at what cost? Can different sets of constraints be described, and what are their implications?

Higher authority (if it is responsible for having defined the constraints in the first place) is challenged. The programmed solving procedures can be turned to good use by showing what opportunities can be revealed when certain constraints are relaxed, and higher authority must eventually give way and concede that such questions may and indeed should be asked, if the defined objectives will thereby be better served.

The curious effect of programmed solution procedures, which higher management prescribes or with which it acquiesces, is that they rebound on higher management itself. They start by depriving lower management of discretion, and then in an attempt to regain discretionary responsibilities, lower management reacts by invading the domain of aims and means, a domain that higher management tries to preserve for itself.

Constraints are a function of the management hierarchy. The higher we go, the fewer the constraints and the less rigidly they are defined. Each level in the management hierarchy is given a set of constraints from a higher level and in turn generates a set, usually more narrowly defined, to the lower level. As we descend the management ladder we find that the framework within which solutions may be sought rapidly diminishes in scope, and with it the area of discretion. And when the method of searching for a solution is itself made a routine procedure, this area of discretion contracts even further. There are only two ways in which the lower echelon can resist these attempts to encroach on its preserve: one is to prove that the proposed solution procedure is not efficient or effective, the other is to relax the domain of constraints.

The first is a more difficult battle, because by the time a solution procedure is proposed it has usually undergone several phases of testing and scrutiny, but there is evidence that some failures of OR projects do occur at the implementation stage and not for reasons of inadequacy of the analytical tools involved. There are also some known examples where OR solutions have been 'successfully' implemented, only subsequently to erode and eventually disappear without trace. Several explanations can be suggested for this phenomenon; one contributory factor could be the reaction of the management level concerned; it tries to reassert its right to participate more actively or to undertake the search-for-solution function.

But the second reaction, namely that of attacking the constraints, may be even more effective, because (as we have seen) it employs the same arguments that have led to the introduction of prescribed search-for-solution procedures. If the lower echelon is to abandon prevailing methods and adopt what is claimed to be a more efficient method, then by the same token why should the higher level not abandon the definition of constraints, if such a relaxation can prove to be beneficial? There are several ways in which the higher level can react to such pressure:

1. behave in an authoritarian manner and refuse to re-examine constraints;
2. relax the constraints and allow more participation of the lower level in defining constraints and decision areas;
3. eliminate the lower level and take over its responsibilities, or dissipate its functions;
4. resist moves to over-prescribe search-for-solution methods and safeguard a reasonable area of discretion for the lower level ('keep the lads occupied; it will keep them out of mischief');
5. substitute areas of discretion which have been eliminated (or are in danger of being so) by new areas ('job enlargement').

CONVERSION OF RESOURCES

Constraints are usually specified as if they were mutually exclusive. This is obviously fallacious. Constraints relate to different segments of the environment in which activities are planned and controlled, and there

must be some trade-offs between them. Consider the main headings under
which constraints may be listed:

market—constraints describing demand, price, competition, terms of
sale;
product (or *service*)—design specifications (including standardisation),
quality (including dependability and reliability), obsolescence and
perishability, variety, cost;
technology—know-how of production (or service) methods, technical
limitations of processes and materials, skill;
organisation—demarcation of functions, product divisions, procedures;
resources—finance, men, machines and equipment, materials, space and
all these are projected against the time dimension, which imposes additional limitations (delivery dates; time lags in procurement, in production, in acquisition of equipment).

But these constraints are not entirely independent of each other:
relaxation of design specifications may have repercussions on quality
specifications, on machine capacities, on costs; shortage of labour may be
overcome by mechanisation and automation; and so on. Particularly in
the case of resources we have to recognise that conversion of one resource
to another in the long term is certainly feasible, but it may also be possible
in the short term.

And yet, as we descend the management ladder we find that constraints
are separately defined. The nearer we approach the operating level, the
more specific they are. They emanate from different sources, from line
management and from various functions, some are more restrictive than
others, some are overlapping. Probably because many constraints are
generated independently by various authorities, there is a tendency to regard them as separate independent entities and even within the realm of
resources we often find each resource being separately defined ('use only
available machines, employ certain types of labour for certain jobs, do not
use overtime, use materials of given specifications', and so on).

To state the constraining resources in an allocation model, such as the
one described earlier, is to some extent to prejudge the issue, to prejudge it
in the sense that the break-down by higher management of the totality of
resources into a plurality of sets of constraints (a set for each resource)
may not be the optimal break-down that can be obtained in terms of the
stated objective function. Admittedly, this break-down may be related to a
different time scale in the decision process than that involved in the allocation model. Take, for example, an allocation problem in production that
needs to be solved on a daily or weekly basis. The constraints pertaining
to machine capacity and labour availability may be due to decisions in-

volving the conversion of facilities that has taken place some time ago, and a complete reappraisal of these constraints cannot be carried out on a short term basis. Nevertheless, the listing of endogenous constraints as mutually exclusive provides the operating echelon of management with a powerful weapon in its attempt to regain a lost domain of discretion.

It would be interesting to observe how this conflict between various management strata develops as information systems become more computerised and as prescription in solution methods increases, and to see how this conflict is resolved.

CONSTRAINTS AT THE TOP

As delegation of authority and discretion at any given level of management may be described in terms of the amount and form of prescription assigned to that level, and as constraints constitute an important ingredient in some forms of prescriptions, our discussion tended to concentrate on those constraints that are imposed by a higher echelon of management on a lower echelon. But this is not to say that constraining in reverse does not occur. In fact it does occur, and it occurs precisely when the higher echelon specifies for the lower echelon control mechanisms that involve discretionary instructions, and when unspecified instructions (see page 169) tend to be interpreted as allowing discretion. If these areas of decisions are truly delegated, they preclude freedom of action by the higher echelon. The room for manoeuvre by a given executive may be crudely represented by a set of cases, like the example described in Table 8.1. If, as suggested earlier, this set S is then divided into four subsets with respect to instructions given to subordinates, (S_1—mandatory, S_2—permissive, S_3—discretionary and S_4—unspecified), then the freedom of action for the executive may be described as having shrunk from S to at least $S - S_3$ and in some circumstances even to $S - (S_2 + S_3 + S_4)$. It is only the components of set S_1 (and in particular those instructions in S_1 that state 'if situation x arises, refer this matter to me', or 'do not handle problems in field y') that are specifically left within the senior executive's domain, and this minimal set is of course augmented by those parts of S_2 and S_4 for which there is a tendency (though not compulsion) for the subordinate to refer to his superior, or for consultation and joint decisions to be undertaken.

Throughout this discussion we must not confuse freedom of action with responsibility. The delegation of discretionary powers to a subordinate does not necessarily imply devolution of responsibility, and this dichotomy is often a source of added frustration to the constrained executive, who is held responsible for actions of his subordinates.

7+

CONSTRAINTS IMPOSED BY FUNCTIONS OF MANAGEMENT*

So far we have examined constraints imposed vertically, by one echelon of management on another. But constraints are also imposed horizontally, by one function of management on others. Thus, the production function is constrained by the sales function as to output targets; by the engineering function as to the design and specifications of the product and as to the processes that can be employed; by the personnel function as to the way in which manpower can or cannot be utilised. And all these constraints are very much a function of time, the short term ones being naturally far more rigid and unalterable than those relating to the long term.

If we examine the effect that a demarcation of functions has on areas of discretion and responsibility in, say, a manufacturing enterprise, we may find a picture as described in the example in Table 8.4.

This is, of course, a rather crude picture. For one thing, I have not defined what is meant by 'short term' and 'long term'. Also, the time allowed for execution in the short term may vary greatly from industry to industry, and even from product to product. A firm establishing a daily newspaper will have its short term measured by a day, or even in hours; a firm publishing text books will measure it in months. Purchasing is depicted in this example as being concerned only with short term problems, but in some industries arrangements for the supply and price of raw materials may have to be agreed a long time before shipments take place. Also, long term may vary greatly from function to function within the same organisation, or even from task to task within the same function. Table 8.4 cannot, therefore, be regarded as more than a qualitative example. Nevertheless, it serves its purpose in highlighting several issues.

1. There is a fundamental difference between discretionary powers and their associated problems that relate to the short term and those that are of a long term character.

2. Some functions in Table 8.4, such as purchasing, even sales and production, are primarily concerned with short-term planning and control; others, like engineering or R and D, are devoted to the solution of long-term problems. This is not to deny the fact that sales and production do pay some attention to the long term (as indeed specifically stated in the table), or that engineering and research need to handle *ad hoc* queries in a hurry (these tasks are often ancillary to the primary responsibilities of these functions, hence no mention of the short term is made in the table), but a fundamental difference between functions does exist in terms of the time span of their discretionary responsibilities.

* I am indebted to Professor Bela Gold for a useful discussion on this section.

3. The discretionary area of each function precisely reflects the constraints it imposes on the other function, certainly in the short term.

4. In the long term each function tends to regard the constraints imposed by others as less binding and may feel more free to challenge

TABLE 8.4   An example of discretionary areas

Function	Short term	Long term
Sales	Price; promotion	New markets; new products*
Finance	Loans	New issues, dividends
Engineering	—	Specifications of new products (and materials); new processes and equipment
Personnel (a) staff	—	Career planning; management development; salaries
(b) operators	Recruiting from labour market; labour relations	Apprenticeships and training schemes; wage structure
Production	Use of given resources	New equipment*; layout and space
Purchasing	Price of materials	—
R and D (research and development)	—	New products, materials, processes
		* Minor role, compared with that played by another function

them. But because of limited competence in other areas, and because these constraints correspond to different time spans, the success of such a challenge is bound to be limited, unless it is combined with or follows a change in organisation structure. An example of the distribution of decision time spans is shown in Table 8.5, from which it would seem that as long-term decisions commit the organisation to widely varying time periods, it is rare for there to be a time when the organisation is free from future commitments and at which a completely unconstrained analysis of future activities can be undertaken.

TABLE 8.5　An example of a distribution of decision time spans

Function	Area	Time Span
SALES	price	├──┤
	promotion	├──┤
	new markets	├──────────┤
FINANCE	loans	├────┤
	new issues	├────────┤
	dividends	├────────┤
ENGINEERING	product design	├──────────────┤
	processes and equipment	├──────────────┤
PERSONNEL (a)	planning for staff	├──────────────┤
	labour recruitment	├──┤
(b)	labour relations	├──┤
	training	├──────────┤
	wage structure	├──────┤
PRODUCTION	use of resources	├──┤
	work study	├──────┤
	layout and space	├──────┤
PURCHASING	price of materials	├──────┤
R AND D	products	├────────────────┤
	material, processes	├────────────────┤

├──▶ time (not to scale)

|◄──────────────────►|◄──────────────────►|
short term　　　　　long term

CONCLUSION

Delegation and areas of discretion enjoyed by any management echelon are determined by the amount of prescription from above and by the nature of the constraints imposed vertically by a higher echelon and horizontally by one function on another. Prescription may be defined in terms of the four types of instructions (mandatory, permissive, discretionary and unspecified) and varying degrees of prescriptions are possible. All prescriptions can be presented in the form of decision tables.

The imposing of constraints by one executive on others (vertically or horizontally) emanates from (a) constraints that have been imposed on this executive by others, and (b) his desire to retain an area of discretion for himself. This area of discretion may be measured by the difference between the constraints imposed upon him and those he imposes on others.

Search-for-solution procedures may be regarded as important ingredients of the discretion area. But when these procedures are specified and when they lead to unique solutions, they cease to represent any discretionary privileges, except perhaps by name.

Constraints imposed horizontally reflect the organisation structure and the time periods for which various functions commit the organisation with their decisions. As these time periods vary greatly, there is less room for manoeuvre in reviewing and relaxing these constraints, than with vertically imposed constraints.

REFERENCE

1. Eilon, S. (1979) *Aspects of Management*, Pergamon Press, Chapter 21.
2. Simon, H. A. (1960) *The new science of management decision*, Harper, New York.

9 Goals and Constraints

In the previous chapter an allocation problem is cited in which a single objective function is to be optimised, subject to meeting certain pre-specified constraints. In examples of this type the specification of the goal appears to be clear: the manager is required to maximise the utility expressed in the objective function, and if the problem is amenable to solution through the use of an appropriate algorithm, the manager is expected to follow the rules of the algorithm in order to obtain the solution to his problem. If the problem is well defined, if the objective function and the constraints are specified, and if an algorithm for a solution is given, the decision process becomes highly prescriptive and impersonal, and the outcome is then expected to be the same, whoever is put in charge of the managerial function.

But as already indicated in Chapter 7, there are many managerial problems which are not highly structured and for which higher authority is unwilling or unable to define a single objective in the form which we have come to expect, say, in a mathematical programming model. The unwillingness or inability of management to do so may stem from difficulties in reconciling various objectives and in reducing them to a single measure through the specification of trade-offs, or it may stem from uncertainties about the validity of the model to describe the behaviour of the system. In either case, the definition of goals, in terms of 'maximise x subject to y' is often totally inappropriate; in some cases it may even be a positively dangerous procedure to follow.

It appears, therefore, that the specification of managerial goals may assume one of two modes.

1. *Optimising*—when the executive is required to act in such a way as to maximise or minimise the value of a predetermined measure of performance.
2. *Satisficing*—when the system is required to perform within given bounds in relation to one, or more commonly several, criteria.

The concept of optimisation has played a central role in the philosophy and development of operational research for many years. It is the epitome of *economic man*: if you want to solve a managerial problem, first state your objective; if there are several, then state your preferences, and if you are forced to be specific enough about your preferences, a comprehensive set of trade-offs can be established from which a utility function will emerge; then exclude from your considerations all the strategies that for one reason or another cannot be implemented, and this is conveniently expressed by a set of constraints; having now defined the feasible choices which are open to you, and having explicitly stated the utility that you wish to maximise, proceed to determine that alternative which is superior to the others in terms of its utility value.

The simplicity and the logic of such an approach are naturally attractive, but by definition it can only apply to well-structured and well-defined problems, and as we have already seen, such problems are amenable to prescriptive decision processes.

There is, of course, a great deal of scope for management scientists in this area of defining and structuring problems. The contributions of operational research in the past two decades have resulted in analytical tools becoming available to assist in the formulation of objectives and procedures in a variety of managerial functions. And in the process of their investigations the management scientists encounter activities which can be defined clearly, which can be structured and which may therefore result in formalised and prescriptive procedures.

But there are numerous functions of the executives that cannot be formalised in this way and for which it is impossible—at least at present—to specify a composite utility. And this is where optimising gives way to satisficing. Simon[1] links this phenomenon with his concept of limited or bounded rationality:

> *The central concern of administrative theory is with the boundary between the rational and the non-rational aspects of human social behavior.* Administrative theory is peculiarly the theory of intended and bounded rationality—of the behavior of human beings who *satisfice* because they have not the wits to *maximize*.

And Simon goes on to say:

> While economic man maximizes—selects the best alternative from among all those available to him—his cousin, whom we shall call administrative man, satisfices—looks for a course of action that is satisfactory or 'good enough'.

Defining goals as satisficing is particularly useful in the case of multi-objectives.* Consider the example cited in Figure 7.5, in which the average

* I have discussed this problem at some length elsewhere.[2]

stock holding Q has an effect on the incidence of stock runouts R in satisfying demand for a given product: the higher the average stock level, the
higher the level of protection against running out of stock. A satisficing
policy for this problem could be described as follows (see Figure 9.1).
Determine the required stock level, such that the incidence of runouts
does not exceed R_1 and the average stock level does not exceed Q_2. In this
formulation no trade-off needs to be stated in utility terms between the

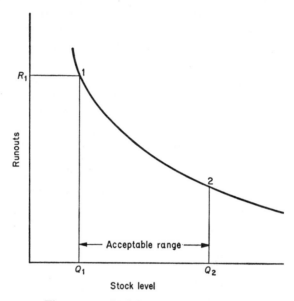

Figure 9.1   Satisficing two objectives

average stock level and the incidence of runouts. Provided the two objectives of having no more than Q_2 and no more than R_1 are not in contradiction with each other, the decision maker has a range of choices within the
interval 1–2 that satisfy the requirements. If the stock level corresponding
to R_1 is Q_1 and if Q_2 corresponds to R_2, then no conflict between the two
objectives occurs if $R_1 > R_2$ and $Q_2 > Q_1$ and any value of Q between
Q_1 and Q_2 is feasible and equally acceptable. Within this feasible set the
decision maker may prefer certain values to others, but such preferences
must be covered by criteria other than the measures in which the problem
has been defined.

CONSTRAINTS

In business situations the formulation of goals by satisficing rather than
by optimising is very common: increase turnover by at least $x\%$, net

profit by at least $y\%$ and reduce man-hours per unit of product by at least $z\%$—such statements are encountered only too often. As long as the minimum levels of performance are attained on all counts, the overall goal is considered to have been achieved.

A close examination of the way in which objectives are defined in a problem of satisficing reveals that these objectives are identical to constraints in a problem of optimising. Take a problem of optimising and remove the objective function and other expressions concerned with descriptions and trade-offs and you are left with a problem of satisficing. Thus, every problem of optimising has an element of satisficing, as described by the constraints, and the need to observe these constraints is just as demanding and as purposeful as the need to achieve the objective specified in a problem of satisficing.

The conclusion to be drawn from this discussion is that the distinction between goals and constraints is an artificial one. That this is the case in a satisficing problem is obvious enough, but even in a problem of optimising the constraints may be regarded as an expression of management's desire to have minimum attainments or levels of performance with respect to various criteria. *All constraints are, therefore, expressions of goals.*

Take the example of a transportation model, for which a suitable cost matrix can be defined. Let there be m sources which supply a commodity to n destinations. If x_{ij} is the amount to be transported from source i to destination j at a cost of c_{ij} per unit, then the objective function is stated as

$$C = \sum \sum c_{ij} x_{ij}$$

which is the total cost of transportation. If A_i is the maximum capacity or amount of available goods at source i $(i = 1, \ldots, m)$ and B_j is the minimum amount required at destination j $(j = 1, \ldots, n)$, then the transportation problem is conventionally defined as follows: Determine the values x_{ij} such as to minimise C, subject to the constraints A_i and B_j. In fact, the problem may be regarded as having not a single objective (to minimise C) but $m + n + 1$ objectives: m objectives pertaining to m sources, n objectives pertaining to n destinations, and one objective associated with costs (there is, of course, the additional requirement that $x_{ij} \geq 0$).

For source i, for example, the capacity constraint is generally expressed as

$$\sum_{j=1}^{n} x_{ij} \leq A_i$$

7*

and as the amounts x_{ij} cannot be negative in value, it follows also that

$$\sum_{j=1}^{n} x_{ij} \geq 0$$

It may be said that the capacity utilisation of source i is subject to two bounds, it must be between 0 and A_i. All allocation problems may, therefore, be formulated in what has become known as *interval programming* terms, where the use of resources or the satisfying of requirements is bounded from both ends. Thus, in the transportation problem a general statement about the capacity utilisation of source i would be

$$A_i' \leq \sum_{j=1}^{n} x_{ij} \leq A_i''$$

where A_i' and A_i'' describe the minimum and the maximum bounds respectively. The specification of a lower limit reflects a commitment that management wishes to make with respect to a minimum level of activity at source i, in other words it is an expression of management's objective to guarantee this minimum. The upper bound, which is often associated with limitations dictated by physical facilities, is again a statement of an objective. Clearly the smaller the interval between the lower and the upper bounds, the fewer feasible solutions are available.

SOLUTIONS

One major difference between a problem of optimising and one of satisficing is that we generally expect the former to yield a single solution which is the best within a feasible set, while the latter has to have the many solutions that comprise the feasible set. It is, of course, possible to construct a problem of optimising, for example in linear or in integer programming, which has several solutions, and similarly a problem of satisficing may be so defined as to have only a single solution, but these are extreme examples. For either type of problem the number of feasible solutions entirely depends on the number and on the nature of the constraints. The more severe they are, the less room for manoeuvre is left to the decision maker. And if they are severe enough, no solution may be feasible at all.

It should perhaps be pointed out that there are many optimisation problems which have clearly determinable mathematical solutions, but the solutions turn out to be quite insensitive to the value of various parameters. Let me mention here two examples. The first relates to the cost of production and inventory holding. The total cost function expressed in terms of processing a batch of product is sometimes found to be quite flat in the vicinity of the optimal batch quantity Q_m (see Figure 9.2). Mathematically the point Q_m may be unambiguously determined, but the fact that substantial deviations from it are likely to have only a very marginal effect on the cost implies that from a managerial control standpoint such deviations may be considered allowable. The resultant increase in cost due to deviations from Q_m may be of the same order of

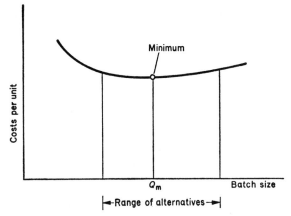

Figure 9.2   Satisficing *vs* optimising for an insensitive objective function

magnitude of (or even lower than) the cost fluctuations resulting from errors or uncertainties in determining the value of the parameters that are fed into the cost function. Under such circumstances it may be reasonable to abandon altogether the optimising of the cost model and to revert to a satisficing model.[3]

The second example relates to the need to determine the magnitude of a controlled variable that can take only integer values. Suppose that the problem is to determine the minimum size of a truck fleet for a given array of tasks (e.g. supplying given consignments to given customers) and suppose that the optimal solution to the problem is to have N trucks. The same solution often applies not just to the given array of tasks, but to many other arrays. Even if the load on the fleet increases (more consignments, or more customers, or both), it is possible that N remains the minimum number of trucks required, until the load increases to such an extent that $N + 1$ become necessary. But when demand declines or fluctuates and a corresponding change at short notice in the size of the fleet is not feasible, then the problem that the manager of the fleet has to face is that of meeting the demand with the available number of trucks.

Thus the problem becomes that of satisficing: allocate the tasks to the trucks such that no more than a given number (say N) are needed.

In industrial and business situations it is common to find goals defined as satisficing constraints, where the constraints progress and become tighter and tighter in the course of time. In the inventory example in Figure 9.1 this could take the form of specifying progressively lower values for R and Q, so that if in period $k + 1$ the constraint for R is $R(k + 1)$, compared with $R(k)$ in period k, then the tightening up process is described by

$$R(k + 1) \leq R(k)$$

and similarly $\qquad Q(k + 1) \leq Q(k)$

The result is shown in Figure 9.3, in which the top line represents the allowable average stock level expressed by the constraint $Q(k)$ and the bottom line gives the minimum average stock level corresponding to the

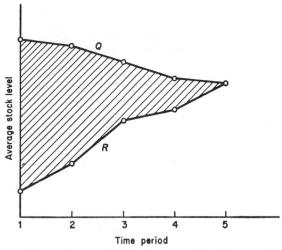

Figure 9.3   Contracting area of discretion

constraint $R(k)$. The distance between the two lines shows the feasible set of solutions, namely the area of discretion available to the manager. As the constraints are redefined each period becomes progressively tighter, this area of discretion contracts, until none may be left. In the example shown in Figure 9.3 the manager is left with a single course of action in period 5, and any further tightening up will result in his being unable to comply with the requirements.

This inventory example is, of course, a very simple one. It involves only two constraints, and furthermore the relationship between them is clearly specified. In any multi-constraint situation, particularly if it lacks such clear relationships between the constraints, the problem is essentially the same. Each constraint represents a minimum required level of performance, and as it is raised, the feasible set of solutions contracts and with it the area of discretion of the manager in charge shrinks as well.

This tendency for levels of performance to become more demanding with time can be figuratively described as the *crawling peg phenomenon*. The constraints are pegged at a certain level and this peg tends to crawl in a given direction. How does this phenomenon come about?

Of the many possible reasons that spring to mind the first is competition. With improved performance of competitors there is bound to be increasing pressure to utilise resources more efficiently and to meet the competition squarely. The tightening of constraints and the specification of more demanding targets is then a natural outcome of such pressure. The use of inter-firm comparisons for control purposes is, in fact, an indication of this effect of competition. If one firm succeeds in reducing costs, or in diversifying, or in improving its level of service to its customers—then immediately its performance becomes a yardstick against which other firms in the same industry or in the same environment are measured. In the absence of inter-firm comparative studies, each firm is somewhat uncertain as to what aspirations in terms of performance criteria would be appropriate and realistic, and it can then only rely on an analysis of data associated with its own past performance. With inter-firm studies, however, there is always pressure, even an obligation, to do as well as the competitor, with the result that standards and objectives are constantly adjusted and become progressively more demanding.

A second reason for the crawling peg phenomenon is the desire of higher authority to have a better control of the system. If manager A specifies to his subordinate B certain goals and constraints that B finds very easy to comply with, then A may feel that he is unable to exercise as much control as he would like. B appears to be meeting the targets quite happily, he does not complain, he does not come to A with his problems. What more natural for A (unless his objective is to have a quiet life) than to try to become more involved in the control process by adjusting the goals? When B begins to scream often enough and loud enough, and provided these screams are justified, then A begins to realise that the slack has gone out of the system. He becomes more involved in determining together with B what courses of action are still open and a coalition between

A and *B* is then formed *vis-a-vis* higher authority to resist further advances of the crawling peg.

A third reason for this phenomenon is the natural desire of man to experiment. The setting up of targets is a form of a test for the system. The uncertainties and complexities of industrial and business systems and the serious penalties associated with their complete failure are such that man is loath to subject such systems to very severe tests. It is safer to design a progression of tests for a system, each more demanding than the previous one, each increasing one's confidence in the ability of the system to perform satisfactorily, each allowing a graceful retreat when difficulties arise without incurring the risk of a complete breakdown.

STANDARDS

The question now arises: how is a manager's performance to be evaluated? And what is the manager's own interpretation of such an evaluation?

In the case of an optimising objective the answer appears to be quite clear: the level of his achievement can be measured by the degree to which the system approaches its optimum performance, if this optimum can be determined. If there are specified algorithms for finding the optimal solution, and if the problem is highly structured (namely if the decision process is prescriptive), then the manager is deemed to behave correctly if he follows the rule-book and incorrectly if he does not. The standard for his performance is determined by the prescription. If he follows the prescription and the system fails to achieve the expected results, he cannot be held responsible.

In the case of a satisficing objective, the setting up of performance standard takes the form of control limits. For example, when a designer specifies a physical dimension on an engineering drawing he indicates a particular value which should be aimed at and he also gives some tolerances above and below this value. Thus, a specification for a shaft diameter of 1·000″ ± 0·020″ means that the designer would like the shaft to have a diameter of 1·000″, but he is prepared to tolerate any value between the two limits 0·980″ and 1·020″.

There are two considerations that determine these specifications.

(1) Based on his technical knowledge, the designer makes an assessment of the way in which the dimensional tolerances of the shaft are likely to affect its performance and the performance of the assembly to which it belongs, and he then announces that in his judgment the specification 1·000″ ± 0·020″ is necessary to safeguard these performance criteria.

(2) The machine tools in the machine shop are capable of producing components to a given level of accuracy, which entails a certain dimensional variability.

If the requirements described in (1) are not in conflict with what can be achieved in (2), the specification (1) prevails. If a conflict does occur it needs to be resolved by resorting to one or several of the following courses of action:

relax the tolerances in (1);
improve the accuracy of the production facilities in (2);
use 100 per cent inspection to eliminate from the finished machined components all those that do not comply with (1).

The use of control charts in quality control illustrates the way in which (2) can be considered through the specification of dimension limits. While in a technical drawing the designer indicates the limits that he believes would be needed in order to safeguard the standard of performance of a component, in a quality control chart the limits are determined by an analysis of past behaviour of the process. After the limits have been established, data on current performance of the process are recorded. As long as the data fall between the control limits, the process is said to be 'under control', but when results violate the control limits, the process is 'out of control' and a corrective action to adjust the process or its input is called for.

The control of any specifiable parameters in processing essentially follows the same pattern. Common examples include the control of pressure, temperature, rates of flow of materials, properties of input materials and finished goods, processing times, costs. Each standard consists of defined double limits between which the system is expected to operate and which represent interval constraints. In some cases a standard of performance is expressed by a single upper or lower limit. For example the number of defectives allowed in a consignment of components would be denoted by some given upper bound and such specifications represent the basis for sampling procedures in quality control; similarly, cost standards are described in terms of upper bounds.

In each case the controller has in front of him specified standards and he proceeds to compare the performance of the system with these standards. *As long as the standards are not violated, the controller does nothing. It is only when the standards are not met that he acts.*

Take the example of production targets. The production controller compares the output of a production system with the target. Even when this target is expressed as a single figure the controller is usually allowed some leeway in interpreting it. Thus, if the target is, say, 100 units of product per day, he may be able to tolerate 99 or 98, or perhaps even a lower production figure; but when the production rate falls below the lower limit (or when the cumulative shortage over a period of time exceeds a given value) he feels obliged to act: he talks to the foreman, he examines the machines, he scolds the defaulters, he complains about the raw materials, he crosses swords with the inspectors. There is, of course, no need for him to do any of these things when production targets are met..

REWARD AND PUNISHMENT

An interesting and important feature of control procedures of this kind is that they are more conducive to the imposition of punishments than to the offering of rewards. When a controller acts it is because the system is in some way unsatisfactory. In formalised procedures in quality control, for example, no provision is made for rewards for good performance. Indeed, good performance is taken for granted, as clearly specified by the standards, whereas bad performance (i.e. the violation of standards) is singled out for taking action. To introduce rewards into the system, explicit arrangements have to be made, explicit because good performance does not require the intervention of the controller in making appropriate adjustments to the system; and in the absence of a conscious effort to reward good performance, it often goes unnoticed.

Another important aspect of control procedures is that *almost invariably standards are determined on the basis of past performance.* In quality control of physical dimensions of a component, for example, samples from the production line are examined and the results are analysed with the view of establishing the variability of dimensions that is associated with the production process. This performance is then interpreted as the level of variability that would be acceptable in future. As mentioned earlier, if the design engineer is not satisfied with these results, then either the components have to be subjected to 100% inspection to segregate the good pieces from the defects, or the production process has to be replaced. Similarly, in specifying production targets, processing times, or performance ratios, the guiding principle is that such targets have been attained in the past.

In the absence of a clear system of rewards and to combat the phenomenon of the crawling peg, it is not surprising that many managers adopt the strategy of aiming to attain only the absolute minimum requirements, but no better. It is, in fact, in their interest not to do much better, because as soon as they do, their achievements may become the standards of the future. The better one does today, the more slack is taken out of the system and the more difficult it may be to keep up a high level of performance tomorrow. In financial statements and in other periodic reports it is common to find such comparisons as profit for current quarter versus profit for the previous quarter (or profit for this quarter last year), and similar comparisons are made for turnover, sales, costs, production volumes, cost per unit, man-hours per unit, etc. Even if it is not explicitly stated that all such performance measures must improve from one time period to the next the very act of comparing time periods implies that past measures become standards for evaluating current performance.

Faced with a multiplicity of objectives which a manager (or an operator) finds increasingly difficult to satisfy, a hierarchical ordering of the objectives and constraints is bound to emerge. Some may be considered vital for the system to maintain, or for the manager to achieve in order to avert the risk of unpleasant retribution; others may be desirable but not crucial, and failure to attain them may be tolerable. Having ranked the objectives in this way, the manager proceeds to meet the requirements as best he can (or as best he would have his superiors believe that he can), but if certain constraints are violated often enough, they are bound—at least informally—to be relaxed to allow just enough slack into the system to enable the manager to comply with them. At this point some readjustment between a number of constraints may take place, certain constraints becoming tighter while others are somewhat relaxed, thereby allowing the crawling peg process for some of the objectives to continue.

CONCLUSION

Some of the propositions suggested in this chapter may be summarised as follows:

1. Objectives may be stated either as a problem of optimising or as one of satisficing. The former is more amenable to prescriptive control than the latter. Both tend to be more conducive to the meting out of punishments than rewards.
2. There is no fundamental difference between objectives and constraints.
3. Standards of performance are often expressed as objectives on the basis of past performance.
4. Objectives tend to become tighter and more demanding with time.
5. Managers tend to resist this 'crawling peg' process in order to preserve their room for manoeuvre.

REFERENCES

1. Simon, H. A. (1961) *Administrative behavior*, Macmillan, N.Y., 2nd edition, pp. xxiv–xxv.
2. Eilon, S. (1979) *Aspects of Management*, Pergamon Press, Chapters 23 and 24.
3. Ibid., Chapter 25.

10 Structure and Determinism

In a foreword to Simon's book *Administrative behavior* Barnard asks: 'What justifies the belief that general knowledge of administrative behavior or organization is attainable?' and he proceeds to give the following reply:

> A university president tells me that his principal organization difficulty is the 'following which, of course, is peculiar to universities'. He then describes a problem I have encountered a hundred times, but never in a university. I listen to a Commanding General of the Air Transport Corps lecturing on organization problems of that Corps. I have never had military experience, I have read little of military organization, yet I think I understand him almost perfectly . . . Such experience forms the ground for the belief that abstract principles of structure may be discerned in organizations of great variety.

The search for a theory of organisation, for general postulates about the behaviour of enterprises and the interactions of their constituent parts has been the preoccupation of many research workers for many years and this is not just an academic pursuit. A theory of organisation has many practical applications. It can tell us how to design the structure of an enterprise, how to forecast the consequences of any change, and how to counteract undesirable effects by taking appropriate action in time.

The existence or otherwise of an organisation theory is crucial, of course, in discussions about management education. One of the fundamental questions that we have to ask ourselves is whether any lessons learnt in one industry or in one enterprise have any relevance to solving problems in another. It is, in fact, the question of whether management expertise is transferable. If it is argued that every industrial enterprise is different from any other and that its problems are unique at any point in time, then learning from experience is hardly relevant or even possible. But if this is not true, if Barnard's observation about the similarity of management problems in totally different environments is valid, then some lessons learnt in one firm can form the basis of experience that is transferable to other firms, or to students embarking on a career in management. The search for abstract principles that form the body of a theory is based on any generalisations that can be formulated on experience and observations, with the hope that such generalisations will withstand the test of future experience.

What are these abstract principles? I suggest that at least some are imbedded in the realisation that the management activity is essentially a control process. The task of management is to plan and control the activities of an enterprise in order to achieve certain predetermined objectives through the efficient utilisation of available resources. To perform this task in a purposeful way, the management process must consist of the various stages described in Chapter 1 and which may be briefly described as:

  determining goals
  planning
  measurement
  organisation and control procedures
  evaluation of performance and control.

Each ingredient in this process is indispensable: it is impossible to reach meaningful decisions if the goals of the enterprise or of its constituent parts are not defined, nor is it possible to make any evaluation of the way in which activities are carried out, unless plans and signposts are set out with which progress and achievements can be compared. These signposts involve the definition of standards of performance against which actual performance can be evaluated. And this implies that a procedure of measurement must be instituted, so that progress can be recorded, because without measurement no data on performance are available, and without data no evaluation is possible.

At least one abstract principle about organisation theory may therefore be linked with the notion that control and decision-making processes form a central part of the management function and that similarities that may be discernable to us between organisation structures stem from inherent similarities of the *control procedures* that are employed in these organisations.

This is not to say, of course, that all organisations are alike. Far from it. After all, human beings are all made of the same elements and molecules, but each person has his own distinctive characteristics. Similarly, even though the ingredients of the management process are essentially the same in every case, the organisation structure, which provides the framework for the many decisions and control procedures which take place in an organisation, can (and does) assume a variety of forms.

Thus, when we say that we encounter similarities between organisations of the kind mentioned by Barnard, there may be three distinct levels at which these similarities are identified.

1. *At the fundamental control level.* We observe the activities of executives and note common features of the control procedures associated with various tasks in several enterprises.

2. *At the problem definition level.* We talk to executives and try to describe the problems that they have to face and we find that several classes of problems can be defined in abstract but sufficiently specific terms to encompass many problems that executives have to solve in seemingly totally different environments. This is why operational research models of inventory, scheduling, allocation and congestion problems have been formulated in general abstract forms, irrespective of the type of industrial activity with which they can be encountered. A project scheduling problem, for example, may be associated with the building of a bridge, a dam, an aeroplane, an office block or a large turbo-generator. All these problems consist of various activities which are linked in a particular sequence and which require various resources, and all can be planned and controlled through the use of network analysis techniques.

3. *At the organisation structure level.* We find similarities between the structure of enterprises in different industries and this gives rise to speculation about the reasons for such similarities.

Clearly, similarities at any one of these levels are not found to the exclusion of others. When two firms are said to be similar in their organisation structure, similarities in problem formulation and in control processes are bound to be detected as well. The three levels merely reflect the variety of approaches open to the investigator, depending on the questions that he wishes to address himself to.

Not surprisingly, perhaps, many writers and research workers in the field of organisation theory have devoted their attention to similarities in organisation structures. If universal maxims about the practice of management can be postulated—for example, about specialisation of management function according to purpose, time or place, or generalisations about the span of control and the unity of command—then a theory of organisation will begin to emerge. Classical management theory abounds with these maxims—which Simon[1] calls 'the proverbs of administration' and which he proceeds to question on theoretical and semantic grounds. Others have attacked the classical theory on empirical evidence, by studying various organisation structures and then demonstrating that some of the 'proverbs' simply do not stand up to the harsh facts of industrial reality.

VIEWS ON STRUCTURE*

What does the organisation structure depend on? There seem to be two schools of thought on this subject. The first may be described as that of *structural individualism*, the second as *structural determinism*.

Those who believe in structural individualism see the characteristics of an organisation structure as embedded in the personalities of its top executives. These personalities, so it is argued, create a certain managerial style, which in turn determines the design of information channels, the pattern of delegation of tasks and responsibilities, and even the control procedures that are employed. The level of prescription in management decisions is affected not only by the characteristics of the task, but in the main—the followers of this school of thought suggest—by the forcefulness and strength of character of the executives and the extent to which they wish to participate in the decision processes of their subordinates.

Those who believe in structural determinism largely ignore the personalities of individuals but argue that structure is determined by the environment, as suggested in Figure 1.1. The organisation constantly needs to adapt to the needs and the pressures of the environment, hence changes in organisation structures are a manifestation of this process of adaptation. The environment consists of several segments, of which one may prove to be dominant, and then—so it is argued—the structure of the organisation is determined by the dominant segment. If, for example, the market is the dominant factor, the organisation cannot help but become market oriented in its structure, so that the marketing function becomes dominant within the organisation and other functions become partly or totally subservient to it.

It is perhaps easier to find fault with structural individualism than to denigrate structural determinism. The proposition that an organisation structure is entirely dependent on the chief executives ignores the direct interactions between the enterprise and the environment and recognises exogenous effects only through the changes that they bring about in the personalities of the executives, their behaviour and their set of beliefs. Thus, while we cannot deny that individuals can and do affect the well-being and the destiny of enterprises under their control, our experience does suggest that most men are servants and not masters of their environment.

Structural determinism, on the other hand, appeals more readily to

* This issue is discussed at some length elsewhere,[4] see also the *Feedback* section in OMEGA (1978), vol. 6, no. 2.

those who seek to identify the causes and circumstances that lead an enterprise to assume a particular organisation structure. Such a belief is a great encouragement to the empiricists, who wish to look at the world as it is and subject the propositions of any given organisation theory to the test of reality.

The followers of structural determinism do not necessarily adhere to the view that the effect of the environment on the organisation structure is unidirectional, as suggested in Figure 1.1. But even if they accept the counter-effects depicted in the triad model in Figure 1.2, it is reasonable for them to assume that the organisation is likely to react more quickly to changes in the environment than *vice versa*. Within a given time, therefore, the effects would appear to be unidirectional, and the empiricist could attempt to identify the segments of the environment which seem to be most relevant to the purpose of correlating the characteristics of the organisation structure with the prevalence of certain environmental parameters.

This approach is not without danger; an element of tautology can easily creep into the arguments. Take, for example, an enterprise which is found to have marked leanings towards marketing. The size of the marketing department, the status and salary of the marketing-director and his subordinates, the manner in which production scheduling activities are solely determined by the dictates of the marketing men—all these are symptoms which suggest that the organisation structure is market oriented. An investigator now proceeds to seek the reasons for this phenomenon. He questions the executives of the firm about their tasks and about the problems that concern them most, and lo and behold! they seem to be mainly obsessed with what competitors do, with pricing, with advertising, with customer service. The investigator then jumps to the conclusion that the concern of these executives with marketing problems is due to the external environment, in which competition is an all important parameter, and he then records the significant fact that the marketing sector of the external environment has been a dominant factor in the design of the organisation structure of the enterprise. In other words, he is arguing that the organisation structure is market oriented because it is market oriented. Clearly what he must do is to define and measure the causal parameters in a way that is completely independent of the observation and measurement of organisational phenomena, otherwise the validity of statements about causal relationships is bound to be viewed with some scepticism.

THE DEFINITION OF STRUCTURE

One of the fundamental problems that students of organisation structure have is the definition of parameters which characterise a structure. If they follow the classical classification of organisations into line, staff (or functional) and line–staff structures, they are immediately faced with problems of definition of each type. It is extremely rare, for example, to find either pure line or pure staff organisation structures, so that most enterprises inevitably fall into the line–staff category. Alas, this is not very helpful in classifying organisations, so that terms such as 'predominantly line' or 'predominantly staff' have to be introduced and this in turn entails a definition as to what is precisely meant by 'predominant' and how it can be determined.

Other measures that have been considered are the growth of specialist departments, the number of levels in the management hierarchy, the span of control of the chief and other executives, the ratio of operators to first-line supervisors, the ratio of managers to other staff, the ratio of direct to indirect labour, and so on. No doubt all these parameters are relevant to the description of an organisation, but a mere list of parameters—even if one is reasonably assured that their definitions are impeccable and that methods of measuring them are not in dispute—does not constitute a classification of organisation structures. At best, such an approach allows each parameter to be considered in isolation. Thus, we can study firms A and B and observe that they have similarities in the ratio of staff graduates to non-graduates, or that they are very different in their ratios of direct to indirect labour. Can we make inferences from such data about *similarities* or dissimilarities of the *structure* of the two firms? To categorise organisation structures there is a need for *a set of attributes*, and needless to say each must be unambiguously defined. It is at this fundamental level that empirical studies concerned with establishing causal relationships between the structure of the enterprise and the environment fail to provide the necessary conceptual framework which would allow such relationships to be examined.

For example, some investigators who may be regarded as belonging to the school of structural determinism have identified technology as the major segment of the environment and argue that if technology is classified into several categories according to the type of production (such as mass, batch or job production) then a correlation can be found between the type of production and type of organisation structure. Summarising their studies of various firms they conclude that 'firms with similar production systems appeared to have similar organisational structures',[2] but what was in fact found was that the mean or median of a particular attribute (say, the number of levels of management, or the ratio of staff to industrial workers) was different for groups of firms in the sample. Even if such observations were to be carried out for a large number of attributes, we still lack the fundamental definition of different types of organisation structures. To say that firms belonging to group A have a different average attribute from firms belonging to group B does not mean that firms in group A have a similar structure. In fact, in the case of almost every attribute it was found that its variance for each group was so wide as to result in significant overlaps between the groups. Furthermore, if similarities in attribute values for firms in a given group were shown to exist, they still would not add up to a description of an organisation structure. What is required is a definition of various types of structure, based on a list of given attributes, and similarly a parallel definition of types of technology, based on a *separate* set of attributes, *prior* to the testing of the hypothesis that a correlation between the two exists. The major thesis of those who believe in technological-structural determinism, namely that technology is a determinant factor in organisation design, suffers from the lack of rigorous definitions, and has resulted—in spite of massive efforts in data collection —in conclusions based partly on arguments which, on closer examination, turn out to be tautological.

The task of providing the necessary definitions is, of course, an extremely difficult one and I confess that I have not yet come across a classification for complete organisation structures which is either meaningful or convincing. An organisation structure is not just a hierarchical pyramid that can be defined by the ratio of its height to its base or by some other global measures. The structure is a framework within which a great number of control procedures have to be accommodated and it is therefore doubtful whether a satisfactory definition of an organisation can be complete without an appended description of the control procedures that are employed. And herein lies part of the difficulty: even if we could identify and record all the individual control procedures in every single department of the organisation, the overall description of control that would typify the organisation structure as a whole must require an integration of the individual localised procedures at a level of sophistication that has so far completely eluded us.

These arguments are not intended to deny that instances in industry can be cited in which the type of production employed may be the major factor in determining the scale of operations and the necessary speed of response by controllers and hence in leading to certain organisational characteristics that need to be adopted, at least in some parts of the enterprise. Sometimes manufacturing operations are entirely dominated by the kind of machines and production processes that—because of prevailing competition in the market—the enterprise has no choice but to employ. It is sometimes possible for machines and processes to dictate not only the scale of operations, but the primary features of the control procedures that need to be used. While such examples should not be overlooked, many instances can also be cited of firms in the same line of business that have evolved organisationally in different ways. The relatively small number of cases in which similarities in structure appear to have been found does not justify the generalisation that any given structure can be directly related to particular technological attributes and that other types of structures could not have been evolved.

STRUCTURAL CHOICE

There is an almost fatalistic flavour to the arguments of some of the believers in structural determinism. The organisation of an enterprise has to adapt to the environment, it has to undergo necessary and inevitable changes in order to withstand new pressures exerted by external agents, or to adjust to new demands generated by technological change. Hence, the structure of the organisation has to evolve in response to all these demands and pressures, so that the structure that we observe at any given time is the result of this process of adaptation. The strict adherents of structural determinism suggest that the organisation must evolve in a particular way and they inevitably assume certain forms which are characteristic of the dominant segment of the environment that has been identified.

This notion of inevitability in the development of the organisation structure appears to deny the proposition inherent in the triad in Figure 1.2 that there are no clear cause and effect relationships here and that each parameter in the triad may cause a change and may in turn be affected by the others. If this proposition is correct, then there is no reason to assume that for given environmental conditions the evolution of an organisation structure, however it may be defined, must necessarily converge towards any one particular form, or indeed follow any particular path. Structural determinists seem to take such a property of convergence for granted, but on what evidence or fundamental arguments?

Perhaps one of the puzzling consequences of structural determinism is the question of structural choice, namely the ability of management to choose between several possible organisation structures. To be a strict believer in structural determinism one would have to conclude that there is no structural choice. If the informal structure is effectively determined by the environment, then no matter what management decides it prefers in this matter, the eventual outcome is predetermined. Even though structural determinists do not state this conclusion explicitly, it represents a familiar dilemma which is an inevitable outcome of a philosophy of determinism.

Again, this is not to deny that in extreme cases environmental parameters can be so overwhelming, for example in terms of competition, that an enterprise can survive only if it is prepared to engage in a certain scale of operations, which in turn could affect technology and organisation structure. But it does not follow that because such cases can be isolated any generalisation for industry as a whole need be valid. I am not suggesting, of course, that structural choice is unlimited and that management is free to choose any structure or any control procedure that it fancies (such a proposition would again deny the effect of interactions such as depicted in Figure 1.2), merely that the evidence for the determinism theory is far from being convincing and that various studies in organisational change suggest that non-gradual changes in organisation structures and procedures—consciously planned—do take place; a close examination of such changes also suggests that, far from each particular change being inevitable, management often has several choices. Lawrence,[3] for example, tells the story of how one company deliberately changed its basic managerial procedures throughout the organisation and adds that 'it is no accident that there exists a widespread management belief that important organizational changes are virtually impossible to carry out in substance as well as in form'. Alas, this widespread belief exists not just in management circles, but also among organisation theorists.

A measure of choice does exist, and it is precisely because it exists that we need to know much more than we do about the possibilities and their consequences on the performance of the enterprise and the behaviour of the people in it. Take, for example, the choice of a function-oriented organisation as opposed to one that is task oriented. The first tends to divide responsibility at the top management level according to such functions as production, sales, personnel, finance and so on. The second tends to have divisions according to product groups. The first centralises services for all tasks, the second integrates authority and decision-making nearer each task. The first enjoys some benefits of economy of scale (it is cheaper to purchase centrally, to market centrally, to have certain central manufacturing facilities), the second enjoys the benefits of men being identified with specific tasks and products.

In large organisations the difference between the two can become very real. The functional-oriented management can develop expertise in particular functions, which become independent entities with a life and a *raison d'être* all of their own, almost completely detached from the rest of the organisation. They can develop into institutions which are reminiscent of government departments. These then issue edicts for overall policies to guide the work of the enterprise, and these policies can take different forms: they can be of a *laissez-faire* type, where top management addresses itself to the problem of creating a suitable environment, the idea being that if the environment is right then every individual in the organisation will react positively, his performance will improve and the whole enterprise will benefit thereby; or they can be restrictive in character, attempting to direct and control from the centre as much as possible and leave the individual to swim or drown in the process.

On the other hand organisation by product group tends to be perhaps more purposeful. The functions of management are more oriented towards the products and tasks of the enterprise and therefore more integrated within each product group. This allows tracking and feedback procedures to be designed so that they can be adaptive; management control can become more decentralised, and time lags in decisions shortened. The product centres become more identified with their own tasks and less identified with the rest of the enterprise, while top management can easily assume the role of a holding company and become rather remote from shop-floor operations.

It is not my intention to extol the virtues of one type of organisation as compared with another, but merely to underline the fact that structural choices may have far-reaching consequences for the enterprise.

Even within a given structure there are many points of detail that have to be filled in, many procedures and mechanisms to be designed, each with several parameters that need to be determined. How relevant and important, for example, is a detailed documentation process? How much paper work should be tolerated? There must be enough of it to provide relevant information for decision makers, but not so much that it causes congestion in the information network, or causes mental indigestion to the executives. How much consultation should be instituted, to provide adequate participation in the control procedures of employees at different levels, without taking too much time? What kind of evaluation methods should be employed and at what frequency, so that they are not so rare as to be ineffective, yet not so frequent as to become stale and again ineffective?

These are just some of the components of the grand design of management control. Indeed some of these components may involve the setting up of special departments with elaborate working procedures, such as computer centres, operational research departments, controllers and expediters. There are many choices which should be adopted in any given situation. What is the right level of expenditure on, say, a computerised information system, on research and development, on operational research? How can we measure the return on this expenditure? And above all, how do we ensure that the organisation has the necessary capabilities of learning and adaptation, as well as the ability to act promptly in cases of emergency?

It is easier to ask these questions than to give general answers. And this in itself is an indication of the inadequacy of the state of our knowledge in this field. The study of organisations is still in its infancy and there is a vast amount of research to be done—both theoretical and empirical—before the many fragmented hypotheses which emerge from isolated studies can be integrated into a unified theory of some substance. I believe that the concepts of decision making and control can be employed as a suitable framework within which such a theory will evolve.

REFERENCES

1. Simon, H. A. (1957) *Administrative behavior*, Macmillan, N.Y.
2. Woodward, J. (1965) *Industrial organization—theory and practice*, Oxford University Press, p. 50.
3. Lawrence, P. R. (1958) *The changing of organizational behavior patterns—a case study of decentralization*, Harvard University, p. i–ii.
4. Eilon, S. (1979) *Aspects of Management*, Pergamon Press, Chapter 3.

Index